SHANE STANFORD
ANTHONY THAXTON

UN*failing*

Stumbling Our Way
into God's Unlimited Goodness

WHITAKER
HOUSE

UN-FAILING
Stumbling Our Way into God's Unlimited Goodness

shanestanford.com
www.thaxtonstudios.online

ISBN: 979-8-88769-324-8 + eBook ISBN: 979-8-88769-325-5
Printed in the United States of America
© 2024 by Shane Stanford and Anthony Thaxton

Whitaker House
1030 Hunt Valley Circle
New Kensington, PA 15068
www.whitakerhouse.com

Library of Congress Cataloging-in-Publication Data
Names: Stanford, Shane, 1970- author. | Thaxton, Anthony, author.
Title: Un-failing : stumbling our way into God's unlimited goodness / Shane
    Stanford, Anthony Thaxton.
Description: New Kensington, PA : Whitaker House, [2024] | Summary:
    "Weaving stories from Scripture, history, and modern times, suggests
    that looking at the other side of failure, viewing it as an opportunity
    to learn and draw closer to God, can result in spiritual growth,
    maturity, and success"— Provided by publisher.
Identifiers: LCCN 2024016381 (print) | LCCN 2024016382 (ebook) | ISBN
    9798887693248 | ISBN 9798887693255 (ebook)
Subjects: LCSH: Spiritual formation. | Failure (Psychology)—Religious
    aspects—Christianity. | BISAC: RELIGION / Christian Living / Spiritual
    Growth | SELF-HELP / Personal Growth / Success
Classification: LCC BV4501.3 .S73115 2024 (print) | LCC BV4501.3 (ebook)
    | DDC 248.4—dc23/eng/20240603
LC record available at https://lccn.loc.gov/2024016381
LC ebook record available at https://lccn.loc.gov/2024016382

1 2 3 4 5 6 7 8 9 10 11 ᴡ 31 30 29 28 27 26 25 24

DEDICATION

For Ronnie,
Thank you for allowing my "wrongs" to be made "right." In Him.
—S. S.

For Amy,
In my weakness, you've made me strong. I love you.
—A. T.

CONTENTS

INTRODUCTION: THANK GOD WE CAN START ANEW

Shane Stanford

If you've followed Jesus for any length of time, we're sure you've found one thing to be true: It's not easy. We fail over and over. We try to do what we think is best, only to completely disregard what God is saying to us. We grow in some areas and really struggle in others. We take three steps forward and two and a half steps back.

This can be a sobering reality for anyone who truly wants to live for God. But the reality is also that we're not alone. The Bible is full of godly people who struggled along the way, people who failed big-time and were then reshaped into who God created them to be.

We believe there is power in examining the lives of some of the Bible's most noteworthy characters. It can be deeply formative to see how their lives were perhaps not so different from our own.

But first, let's talk about you. How do you view failure? Does failure feel like losing? Does it make you believe less in yourself and less in God moving through you? Or do you see failure as part of the process, as a series of steps forward and backward that ultimately take you in extraordinary, world-altering directions?

Theodore Roosevelt once said, "The only man who never makes a mistake is the man who never does anything."[1] Entrepreneur Henry Ford, who invented the moving assembly line, called failure the opportunity to begin again "more intelligently," adding, "There is no disgrace in honest failure; there is disgrace in fearing to fail."[2]

I think most of us see failure as bad. We see two options: winning or losing. To succeed in what we want to do is to win. To fail is to lose. But living in a world with such strict views of winning and losing, success and failure, creates a dynamic of permanence in our failures. We become branded with the results forever. Sure, we share platitudes such as, "It doesn't matter if you win or lose, it's how you play the game," yet so much of our world looks to the win-loss ratio to determine the value of next steps and purpose.

What happens if we begin to see failures, mistakes, and broken periods as chances to begin again?

But what happens if the exception becomes the rule? What happens if we allow the paradigm to shift and begin to see failures, mistakes, and broken periods as chances to begin again? As opportunities to provide world-altering corrections to our course?

OVERCOMING OBSTACLES

Failure frightened me while I was growing up. As a frail hemophiliac, I received tainted medicine and was diagnosed as HIV positive at the age of sixteen. I was given two years to live, but I kept hanging around. Then at

---

1. Jacob A. Riis, "Theodore Roosevelt," *The American Monthly Review of Reviews*, vol. 22, no. 2, July-December 1900, Albert Shaw, ed. (New York: The Review of Reviews Co.), 184.
2. Henry Ford, *My Life and Work* (Garden City, NY: Garden City Publishing Co., 1922), 19–20.

age twenty, I tested positive for hepatitis C. My future looked very different than most kids my age.

Many people with chronic or terminal illnesses—especially those diagnosed very young—agree that life speeds up when you learn of a life-changing prognosis. There is a tendency to give up or to resign yourself to the inevitable.

Thankfully, I never saw my future that way.

I had always been ambitious. I wanted to be the best at whatever I did. I dreamed of success, largely framed by the world's standards. I wanted to be wealthy, accomplished, and recognized. Before my diagnosis, there was no doubt that I wanted to make the most of life. I think most people feel this way at that age. The key was that after my diagnosis, those feelings did not go away. The reality of my situation had changed. I'd been handed boundaries and obstacles that most people would never have to face. Yet I never scaled back my desire to be successful.

I was so determined that my psychologist believed I suffered from denial; he said I had a "staggering sense of optimism in the face of such obstacles." That explanation may have made sense in his note-taking, but I don't believe it was denial. I believe my outlook was the result of the choice I made when confronted by the devastating news that I was not expected to live very long. Despite my diagnosis, my desires did not change. Despite the hardship, obstacles, and all of the things stacked against me, my determination remained the same: I would make something of my life.

What did change was the timeframe and scope of what that *something* could be. It was literally now or never. Either I would begin working on the life I felt called to … or I would waste time and succumb to the inevitable.

A NEW PERSPECTIVE

My body's *failure* offered me a gift that I would never have had under normal circumstances: I received a new perspective. Yes, time sped up. The obstacles were great. The reality of what I believed I could accomplish became stark. But what I learned during those challenges was that winning the race—my old understanding of success—meant far less than having others know why I ran that race with such purpose and fortitude. In other words, I found something more valuable than success: I found perspective in how significant the attempt itself can be.

To date, I have written over fifteen books. I've loved the writing part of my ministry but I never planned to be a writer. Watching friends and colleagues who were (and are) so gifted and skilled as writers, I wondered if I would have enough to say. I wondered if I could possibly say anything that folks would want to read. I found the answer to both of those questions in my personal story. Remember that young sixteen-year-old hemophiliac I mentioned earlier? Well, the stories surrounding all of my many medical struggles continue to fill countless pages. One of my first writing mentors told me, "Write what you know … write as you are!" I am still discovering all that those words mean, but looking back on my books, I see the evidence of that endeavor—to put what I know and who I am down on paper.

I wrote *JourneyWise: Redeeming the Broken & Winding Roads We Travel*, my book about the Beatitudes, after discovering five translations of them on my grandmother's nightstand the morning after she passed away. *When God Disappears*, my reflections on six encounters with Jesus by those who thought they had either *gone too far* or were *too far gone*, developed as the result of an unexpected open-heart surgery in which I was given a fifty-fifty chance for survival. And I wrote *The Five Stones* with a dear friend after we spent an entire lunch talking about giants we had faced or were currently facing.

LEARNING FROM IMPERFECTIONS

Each book was the result of something more than a publishing contract or another line on the resume. They became a continued conversation on paper about something deeper in my work, my walk, or my soul. In pausing long enough while writing this book to ponder the birth of previous ones, I discovered two truths:

1. Imperfection teaches louder and deeper than the opposite

2. We all have lots of imperfections from which to learn

The key to learning what failure, brokenness, or our imperfections have to teach us is this: We build walls around the things we're not proud of. We hide our imperfections, our losses, our bad moments. We pretend they don't exist and do everything we can to convince others of the same.

But what would happen if we turned it all on its head?

What if we weren't afraid anymore? What if those very things we are hiding are the most important cornerstones for our future?

THE OTHER SIDE OF FAILURE

My co-author Anthony Thaxton and I want to take you on a journey to the other side of failure, to guide you into the realm of *un-failing*, as it were. Anthony has been one of my best friends for many years. We've weathered our own share of brokenness, and here, on the other side, there are some places we want to take you. We are getting ready to climb the walls that we've built. And if you're willing, we pray you will allow us to tackle your walls too. It won't be easy or simple. It will cause you to face difficult realities and challenge pretenses that often control your life. It may even anger or frustrate you. We may have to throw your favorite assumptions and perspectives over the wall to get you to follow, but hear me out. It is worth it. On the other side, failure is not a list of wins and losses but the effects and consequences of a life full of true significance—lessons born from the best places and parts of us, even if the circumstances around us are stormy and unsettled at times.

> *Failure is not a list of wins and losses but the effects and consequences of a life full of true significance.*

We don't expect you to simply take our word for it as we go through these redemptive lessons. No, we use examples far beyond our own wisdom and expertise. Over the course of this journey, we will share examples from Scripture of various characters and their stories; we will try to get it right about when they got it wrong. No tricks, no gimmicks. Just one familiar story after another of some of the most important connections we have with the God of the universe as presented in Holy Scripture. (By the way, more often than not, God used the imperfect, tattered side of a person's tapestry to create the picture He most wanted the world to see.) Each chapter will highlight another truth, breakthrough, or balm born only from the failures of our bodies, relationships, or choices, and will be supported by stories of relatable figures in history and encounters in our own lives. In these accounts, we can find great insight into our own experiences and struggles. And, by the end of this journey together, we believe you will see another overarching lesson: if God could use the broken people in the Bible, He can do the same with you!

John W. Gardner, founding chairman of Common Cause, had a friend who asked the same question of almost every new acquaintance: "What have you done that you believe in and are proud of?" It was an unsettling question for many, but the man just wanted honest answers. "I really don't care how they answer," he said. "I just want to put the thought in their minds. They should live their lives in such a way that they have a good answer. Not a good answer for me—for themselves. That is important."[3]

That is exactly what we hope this book does for you. It is easy to give a "good answer" for the good things we have experienced. But we believe there are good answers for the failures too—for the moments when things don't work out, when the loved one is not healed despite our prayers, or when the miracle does not come through to ensure that everyone lives happily ever after. Even in those moments, we believe in a God who, as Paul states, still *"works for the good of those who love him"* (Romans 8:28). We want to give you that arrow in the quiver, that tool in the toolbox, to enable you to look back at the world even on your worst day and say, "God makes beauty from ashes."

Yes, failure is personal, but it doesn't have to control or shame you. There is significance even in these moments. Anthony and I are ready to share some amazing stories with you, so that after each chapter, each lesson, and each story of the seemingly hopeless, you are moved to proclaim, "If God could use them, God can do the same for me!"

So be it!

---

3. Dr. Dale E. Turner, *Different Seasons: Twelve Months of Wisdom and Inspiration* (Homewood, IL: High Tide Press Inc., 1997), 154.

SECTION ONE: FOUNDATIONS FOR UN-FAILING

T homas Edison invented the microphone, the phonograph, the incandescent light, the storage battery, talking movies, and more than one thousand other things. In the 1880s, he spent more than $100,000 (roughly $3 million in today's dollars) to obtain six thousand different fiber specimens, and only three of them proved workable for his experiments. Yet when asked about the seemingly lost investments, Edison said failure brought him that much closer to the solution to his problem. He understood the intrinsic value of failure as a part of the process for accomplishing the most important things in life.

For instance, Edison spent ten years working on a storage battery. The endeavor nearly bankrupted him. One evening in December 1914, a spontaneous combustion broke out in the film room of his plant. Within minutes, all of the packing compounds, celluloid for records and film, and other flammable goods exploded. Fire companies from eight surrounding towns arrived, but they were unable to control the blaze. Everything was destroyed. Edison was sixty-seven. Although the damage exceeded two million dollars, the buildings were only insured for $238,000 because they were made of concrete and thought to be fireproof.

"When I couldn't find Father, I became concerned," said his son, Charles. "Was he safe? With all his assets going up in smoke, would his spirit be broken? He was 67, no age to begin anew. Then I saw him in the plant yard, running toward me. 'Where's Mom?' he shouted. 'Go get her! Tell her to get her friends! They'll never see a fire like this again!'"

Later, Thomas Edison said, "You can always make capital out of disaster. We've just cleared out a bunch of old rubbish. We'll build bigger and better on the ruins."[4]

We are going to fail and we are going to face failure. Each and every one of us. We will surely have our successes, but in between them, we will make mistakes, our bodies will give out, things will happen out of our control, and we will get tired, sometimes to the point of feeling unable to go on. We will get disappointed and sometimes not *want* to go on. This is the nature of life.

The world tells us that success and failure are distinct, laying on two separate ends of a field. They are not. They are two sides of the same coin, and you can't have one without the other. Most importantly, failure is not the end. Often, it is just the beginning of us learning some greater lesson that propels us forward in our lives to greater things. The catch, though, is that we have to accept failure and learn from it in order for that to happen. We can't just fail and stew in our unhappiness. We can't pretend it didn't happen and just charge forward. That doesn't do us or anyone else any good.

4. Charles Edison, "The Electric Thomas Edison," *Great Lives, Great Deeds* (Pleasantville, NY: Readers Digest Association, 1964), 203.

Change and good things happen when we recognize and admit our failure and use it to approach our lives differently. We need to *un-fail*. It's not easy, but we believe you can find hope and inspiration for your own circumstances in the accounts that follow. As you read these and face your own life and your own turmoil, keep in mind that you are not alone. You might stumble, you might lack, or you might make a decision that's absolutely wrong and selfish at some point, but God is with you. *"And we know that for those who love God all things work together for good, for those who are called according to his purpose"* (Romans 8:28 ESV).

As God weaves through our lives, He can take the failures and the successes and ensure they all work together for good.

All things. Not some things. *All* things. Even the bad ones. Even the ones we cringe while remembering. Even the ones that caused us to lose that relationship or that job. As God weaves through our lives, He can take the failures and the successes and ensure they all work together for good, as long as we keep turning back to Him, recognizing our true purpose in Him, and moving forward. With God at our side, we can move past our mistakes and begin to un-fail, begin to let our experiences mold and guide us into wiser and more loving human beings.

Let's begin shifting our perspective and seeing failure for what it is: a part of the process. A part of life, a part of success, a part of learning how to be a better human being, a part of learning what it means to truly follow Jesus.

We're going to start by looking at our foundations for un-failing—the starting point, if you will. How do we see ourselves and our lives in light of what we've done and who we are? How do we start processing and putting into action this idea of un-failing when we've already failed, when we've already hit the walls, overheated our engines, and ground our gears into the dust?

We start by accepting and opening up our hearts to the possibilities of change. Let's get going.

1

LEARNING FROM MISTAKES

(Matthew 26)

Failure can feel like the end, but it's not. When our life falls out from under us, whether due to our own decisions, those of others, or elements entirely out of our control, it can be tempting to either want to go back in time or freeze everything to a standstill until we can resolve whatever we brought into our lives. But going back or making time stand still aren't viable options; we can only go forward.

How do we go about that, though? How do we keep taking steps when we're dealing with the consequences? And how do we deal with the repercussions of other people's poor decisions and selfish natures?

We start by accepting the past. This doesn't mean we have to like it. It doesn't mean we wanted it. Accepting the past means we fully recognize and admit that it happened, we seek forgiveness from God and others if necessary, and we forgive ourselves and others. Only then are we ready to start the process of un-failing. Thankfully, God is with us every step of the way.

THE STORY OF PETER

Peter, one of Jesus's twelve apostles, was shown firsthand what it means to accept what we've done and keep moving, to keep choosing to follow God.

There are few people in Scripture who exhibited the same degree of desire to participate in what Jesus was doing as Peter did. His zeal was intense, and his loyalty to Jesus was strong. When His disciples were in a boat far from land and Jesus appeared, walking on the water, Peter was the one who jumped out of the boat, despite the high winds, and walked on the water toward Him. (See Matthew 14:29.) Peter was also the one who immediately grabbed a sword to protect Jesus when He was being arrested and cut off the ear of one of the men who'd come to take Jesus away. (See John 18:10.) Peter was passionate, to say the least.

And yet, at the Last Supper, he had to sit there with everyone else and listen while Jesus declared, "All of you will abandon Me tonight." (See Matthew 26:31.)

Peter was incredulous. Surely, he'd heard Jesus wrong. There was absolutely no way that Peter would deny this man whom he loved and followed and served.

Jesus did not waver. "The sheep will be scattered," He said. The disciples didn't know what to say. Things were getting serious all of a sudden. Jesus had tried to warn them, had tried to prepare these men for what was about to occur. But now the moment was upon them, and they were at a loss for words.

Peter was outspoken, the bold one. He'd walked on water. He would say something. And he did speak, insisting, "Even if all fall away, Jesus, I never will. I'm with You."

Imagine the chill in Peter's heart as Christ told him, "Before the rooster crows, you will deny Me three times."

Imagine the chill in Peter's heart as Christ simply stared back at him—the rock upon whom Christ would build His church—saying, "Peter, Peter. This very night, before the rooster crows, you will disown Me." Peter was incredulous. It couldn't be true. Betray Jesus? Him? But Jesus wasn't even finished. "You'll deny Me three times," He said.

Peter couldn't believe his ears. Why would Jesus say these things? That would never happen. *"Peter declared, 'Even if I have to die with you, I will never disown you'"* (Matthew 26:35). His words hung in the air. But Jesus knew what was what. He heard Peter's words. He heard the other disciples chime in, saying they would never disown Him either. The dinner had taken a depressing turn, each man determined to somehow change what was coming. No, they never would disown this Man, their Teacher, the Christ.

Jesus led the men outside for a change of scenery, ending up in the garden of Gethsemane. It was a peaceful night, a deceptive prelude to the tragedy that would soon take place. He told His disciples to stay put in the garden while He went to pray, as He was desperate to talk to His Father. He took Peter and two others with him. Three times, He left the men to keep watch as He prayed to the Father, and three times, He returned to find all three men asleep.

"Are you still asleep?" Jesus asked when He returned for the final time. "The hour has come." And indeed, it had. Jesus was delivered into the hands of sinners.

The scene that followed was one of confusion and disbelief, with Jesus bound and taken away by troops from the chief priests and Pharisees. He had not resisted arrest. In fact, He'd told Peter to put down the sword he'd used and healed the man whose ear Peter had cut off. (See Luke 22:51; John 18:10.) Jesus had not proclaimed His innocence or protested in any way. He was suddenly just gone, and the disciples didn't have a clue what to do next.

Peter found himself sitting in the courtyard going over the night's events in his mind. How could he have been so thoughtless as to fall asleep when Jesus had asked him such a small thing, to stay awake and pray? How could Jesus—this King, this Messiah who was here to save and establish a kingdom—have been captured? It was all too confusing. It was frightening, really, and now Peter was alone.

When a servant girl approached and looked him over, she called out, "Weren't you with Jesus of Galilee?" Without thinking, Peter immediately denied it, saying, *"I don't know what you're talking about"* (Matthew 26:70). He quickly walked away toward the gate to leave.

It was an electric night. Everyone in town knew what had happened; everyone was talking. Skepticism and accusations hung in the air. The arrest of the prophet from Nazareth captured everyone's attention.

As Peter hurried toward the gate, he was stopped by another servant girl, who yelled, "Hey, this guy was with Jesus of Nazareth as well."

Peter swore, "I do not know the man!"

He quickened his pace, frantic to escape. It seemed the whole world was crashing down upon him. His head was spinning; his pulse quickened. Then Peter heard it again, yet another voice aimed directly at him. "Surely you are one of Jesus's followers. You have the same accent! It gives you away!"

Peter had endured enough. He began to curse and swear. *"I do not know the man"* (Matthew 26:74 ESV).

Right on cue, a rooster crowed. The words of Jesus at the Last Supper blared in his head: "Before the rooster crows, you will disown Me not once but three times."

Peter's world would never be the same. He went outside the gate and cried bitterly.

If we stopped here, this would be a tragic tale of regret and brokenness and defeat. A tale merely of failure. Which is probably what Peter thought his story would be at this point. There was no chance to make amends, to absolve Peter of his guilt before Jesus's crucifixion. No opportunity to talk to Jesus one-on-one, apologize, make up for it—nothing. Peter soon found himself living in a world where His teacher was buried and gone. The three-year whirlwind of ministry and miracles was over. The curtain had closed. The movement had come to a screeching halt. Peter did the only thing he knew—he went back to fishing, back to his old life. There was nothing left. Fishing was what most of the disciples knew, so instinctively, they returned to the sea. They had to put their minds to rest. They had to do something.

On the day we pick up Peter's story again, in John 21, the men had fished all night but caught absolutely nothing. Imagine how depressing that would be. They had lost their Lord, and now, even the one thing they were pretty good at and had some control over wasn't working for them. As morning broke, they pulled in one empty net after another.

Then a man appeared to them on the shore. He called out, "Friends, have you caught anything?" The disciples didn't recognize Him.

"No," the men grumbled back.

The man called out again, "Just throw your net on the other side of the boat. Then you'll catch some!"

The fishermen groaned. Who was this guy? What did he know? They'd fished all night with no results. But then again, they figured, "We've fished all night with no results." So just for kicks, they threw their net on the other side of the boat.

It was an amazing scene to behold! There were fish everywhere! The net was so full, the men immediately began to try to pull it in and couldn't. It would be quite the fishing story. That's when one of the disciples proclaimed, "It is the Lord!"

Peter froze. The Lord. He almost couldn't believe his ears. Yet with the hordes of fish flopping noisily in the water before him, Peter knew instinctively that it was true. It was Jesus!

Peter dropped the net and jumped straight into the water, swimming to shore to meet Jesus as the other disciples turned the boat to head in.

A campfire burned on the beach, the burning coals just right. Fish and bread cooked over the hot coals. Jesus said to Peter, "Bring some of the fish you've caught." Peter realized he'd left the others to do all the work and went to help bring in the net. It bulged with the huge catch but held fast.

"Come and eat some breakfast," Jesus said to them. So, the disciples ate. They didn't quite know what to say.

As they sat there after the meal, Jesus looked to Peter. Ah, Peter. The rock. Here he was, silent for once. He had no words at all. He'd denied Christ with his voice three times, and now sat mutely before Jesus.

"Simon Peter, son of John, do you love Me more than these?" Jesus asked.

Peter looked at Jesus. "Yes, Lord," he said. "You know I love You."

Jesus said, "Feed My sheep."

The others watched in silence.

Then Jesus asked again, "Simon, son of John, do you love Me?"

Simon Peter answered, "Yes, Lord, You know I love You."

Then Jesus said, "Take care of My lambs."

The sun was rising as warm light bathed their faces. The chill was leaving the morning air.

For the third time, Jesus said, "Simon, son of John, do you love Me?"

Peter could not contain his emotions. It was too much to bear. He was tired from the long night of fishing. In fact, he had been exhausted since Jesus's arrest and crucifixion. Christ had returned, had appeared and disappeared, and had just cooked breakfast for them. And now He was asking Peter for the third time if Peter loved Him.

"Lord, You know everything. You know my heart. You know that I love You," Peter confessed quietly.

Jesus replied, "Then feed My sheep."

A NEW FOUNDATION

All of us betray Jesus at some point or another. All of us make decisions that can hurt Him or the people around us. All of us choose ourselves at His or others' expense every so often when we're under pressure. It is one more way that we will find ourselves failing throughout our lives. And we'll probably wish each time that there was a way to undo what we've done, a way to turn back time and make a different decision. That's probably what had been on Peter's mind since the moment the cock crowed, and he realized his mistake. Unfortunately, there is no rewind, no undo button to go back and erase our mistakes. However, God does provide something else, and we see a beautiful example of it right here, in this moment, on the beach.

> *All of us make decisions that can hurt Jesus or the people around us. All of us long for a do-over to correct our mistakes.*

Because this scene wasn't about the bounty of the catch. It wasn't about the surprising arrival of their Teacher. It wasn't about the return of shared meals, cooked over the fire. It wasn't really even about the other men who were there reconnecting with Christ. Jesus chose this setting, this communion, to redeem Peter. Jesus had prophesied that Peter would turn his back on Him three times. But here, He gave Peter three opportunities to right his wrongs. He offered forgiveness to Peter not once, but three times. As hard as it was for Peter, he had to accept forgiveness from Christ in order to move on and be effective. Jesus gave him a do-over in a way that only Christ could, allowing Peter to move forward from his mistakes.

The challenge for Peter was the same one that confronts many of us. He was left to face the reality of what he had done and how his words, his denial of Christ, had let down someone he loved. The truth was that he really did love Jesus. He really did believe in Him passionately. He made a mistake—three, to be exact—but his mistake brought him face-to-face with his own weaknesses, the very weaknesses that could have prevented him from becoming the person he would eventually be: the rock that God would build His church on. His failure forced him to look at himself and his faults in a way that he never would have otherwise. This gave him a new base, a new perspective, on which he could grow. It would effectively lay the foundation for transforming his life. Because Peter messed up, he was forced to grow and become the person God knew he could be.

A COUNTRY TRANSFORMED

To understand the significance of new foundations born of mistakes, let's look at the historical example of not just a single person but an entire country. The American Civil War remains one of the most momentous events in United States history. It forever changed our nation in many ways, including one noteworthy shift that isn't always discussed: it provided a new perspective for how we view life, death, and the very meaning of our nation.

Drew Gilpin Faust, an American historian and former president of Harvard University, suggests in her book *This Republic of Suffering*[5] that most pre-war communities possessed the same understanding of how death and the afterlife pointed to the overall view of a successful life. The goal of dying at home surrounded by loved ones—citing one's preparation for the end and then slipping gracefully into eternity—was shared by the vast majority of Americans, regardless of geography or social demographics. The idea of such a death was woven deeply into the fabric of what a successful life was supposed to be. It was a framed portrait of existence that brought comfort and meaning during difficult times. Anyone peeking behind the curtain of most neighborhoods or homes knew that not everyone experienced life and its end in such terms. Yet, from pulpits to prisons, the "solemn or beautiful death" promised a glorious tomorrow, even if yesterday and today seemed brutal and cold. Thus, even the most marginalized in society, if they had the right God, showed some sense of confession, and had a loving family around them, could achieve (if even only a portion) the "success" of a good death and eternal life.

After the Civil War, America's notion of a successful life became one that impacted others after death.

---

5. Drew Gilpin Faust, *This Republic of Suffering: Death and the American Civil War* (New York: Knopf Doubleday, 2009).

However, Faust also describes how the nation's view of death and the deeper meanings of life and its purpose changed dramatically in the years following the Civil War. Not only did views change, but the notion of a *successful* ending shifted to conversations about both our responsibilities to one another after we are deceased and our commitments while living. In other words, a successful life became one that continued to impact others long after the person passed away. Faust concludes that none of this conversation, much of which has become the foundation for our deepest considerations of life today, could have happened without such a deeply destructive *failure* as the Civil War. Yes, despite its victories, the Civil War can also be considered one of the country's failures because of everything that led to it and much of what had to happen during it.

It was our failings, our selfishness, and our inability to recognize others' rights and validity as human beings that drove our country to that point. Civil war is a hard, ugly thing. It pits neighbor against neighbor and sends men to die because the country's leaders refuse to come to an agreement. It is the result of hard hearts and people only looking out for themselves.

Was there victory in the American Civil War? Certainly. The North won the war. Were there successes? Absolutely! Slavery was abolished. But any amateur historian knows that Appomattox Court House—where Confederate general Robert E. Lee surrendered to the Union's commanding general, Ulysses S. Grant—was not the end of the story. The effects of the Civil War continued in acute ways for nearly one hundred years after it ended, and it's still affecting the nation in subtle ways today.

But Faust approaches the conversation differently. She concludes that even in catastrophic events such as a civil war, we have much to learn from its most brutal examples and lessons.

Think past the discussion of who won or lost the war. Try to move away from the emotional and personal notations that events such as the Civil War provide. Focus on how even such a truly terrible event changed our lives. For instance, Congress passed the thirteenth and fourteenth amendments to the Constitution, which, respectively, outlawed slavery and granted citizenship and equal protection under the law to all persons born or naturalized in the US. Although it would take another hundred years to tear down most of the vestiges of a racially broken nation, slavery as a possibility in our national culture ceased to exist.

Did racism, violence, and prejudice remain? Certainly—even to this day. But as Civil War historian Shelby Foote suggested, the war changed parts of our consciousness so dramatically that much of what we were beforehand isn't just different; for many Americans, it now seems almost impossible that it was ever so.

LIFE BECAME EASIER, SIMPLER

But it wasn't just the national conversation that changed. The Civil War significantly impacted our nation, our communities, and the world at large. It resulted in the organization of the modern hospital, the embalming process, safer surgical techniques, improved anesthesia, and organized ambulance and nurses' corps. Culturally, the tragedy of the Civil War led to a new understanding of holidays and remembrance, such as the creation of Memorial Day. Additionally, many technological and industrial advances occurred. Fifteen thousand miles of new telegraph lines, reaching all the way to the West Coast, were installed. Mass production of canned food began. Photography took hold as a means of creating legacies and memories of families and loved ones. The need for a transcontinental railroad found a voice. The war also gave us a myriad of devices that changed our daily lives, including can openers, home-delivered mail, differently shaped left and right shoes, ready-to-wear clothing in different sizes, and a national paper currency. All of these made life easier and simpler.[6]

In summarizing the effect of the Civil War on our modern world, Shelby Foote made these observations during Ken Burns' classic documentary, *The Civil War*:

> Any understanding of this nation has to be based, and I mean really based, on the understanding of the Civil War. I believe that firmly; it defined us. The revolution did what it did. Our involvement in European wars beginning with the first World War did what it did, but the Civil War defined us as what we are, and it opened

6. Betsy Towner, "The Civil War: Freedom and 49 other ways it changed American life," *AARP Bulletin*, June 1, 2011, www.aarp.org/politics-society/history/info-06-2011/civil-war-changed-american-life.html.

us to being what we became—good and bad things. And it is very necessary, if you're going to understand the American character in the twentieth century, to learn about this enormous catastrophe in the mid-nineteenth century. It was the crossroads of our being. ... Before the war, it was said "the United States are." Grammatically, it was spoken that way and thought of as a collection of independent states. And after the war, it was always "the United States is," as we say today without being self-conscious at all. And that sums up what the war accomplished. It made us an "is."[7]

Yes, even in the tragic and profound loss of life in the Civil War, even in the terrible circumstances, history, and mistakes that led to it, we found significance amid the staggering evidence that our country was not as invincible as we had perhaps believed. We came out of it with deeper understandings about ourselves, our country, where our brokenness can lead us, and what it means to be one country, indivisible.

Our collective failure to learn lessons from World War I translated into even greater hostilities in 1939.

We are not always so astute. Contrast the American Civil War with the "war to end all wars," World War I. Simply put, our collective failure to learn lessons from WWI translated into even greater hostilities in 1939. Of course, no one would argue that the Allied powers *lost* World War I, but in failing to see past the success of military victory and grasp the real nature of why the war occurred in the first place, they created an even deadlier unraveling two decades later when sixty million soldiers and civilians perished in World War II.

The rise of extreme nationalism, our failure to communicate nation-to-nation, and the unbridled fear of those who are different from us are just a few of the issues that cropped up between 1918 and 1939, costing the

---

7. "Remembering Civil War Historian Shelby Foote," *PBS News Hour,* June 29, 2005, www. pbs.org/newshour/bb/remember-jan-june05-foote_6-29.

world an entire generation. On the other hand, one of the most transformative effects of World War II was the GI Bill, which provided education and opportunities to millions of veterans.

As *New York Times* columnist David Brooks suggests, the essence of any society is how we learn from our mistakes. He notes:

> History is an infinitely complex web of causations. To erase mistakes from the past is to obliterate your world now. You can't go back and know then what you know now. You can't step in the same river twice. So it's really hard to give simple sound-bite answers about past mistakes. The question, would you go back and undo your errors is unanswerable. It's only useful to ask, what wisdom have you learned from your misjudgments that will help you going forward?[8]

NO REDO BUTTON

Looking back at your own history, your own errors and failings, it may be difficult to appreciate the various directions and ways your life may have swerved after those missteps. But remember to acknowledge the change and growth that took place, or the change and growth that *will* happen once you choose to accept that you made mistakes, forgive yourself, and move forward.

Accepting our mistakes and moving forward means changing; it means growing. We have to be ready to shift and take on deeper understanding, knowing that prior decisions transformed everything around us. This is true both of our own actions and those of others, whether they are people currently in our lives or people from the past whose choices still affect us today. We have to be ready for significant change and work with what we are given to make something better out of it.

As you read this book, you might find yourself sifting through your failures, seeking a magic undo or redo of life. It doesn't exist—as hard as that is to admit. Goodness knows we have all prayed and hoped for a mulligan or two many times in our lives. But what *is* in our grasp is deciding what wisdom even our most profound failures can offer us. And we have to

8. David Brooks, "Learning From Mistakes," *New York Times*, May 19, 2015, www.nytimes.com/2015/05/19/opinion/david-brooks-learning-from-mistakes.html.

recognize that what we had before isn't necessarily what we'll have again. Even after forgiveness, even after restoration, we might walk away with very different lives than we had before.

MAKING SOMETHING BEAUTIFUL

Ub Iwerks is not a familiar name to most people. He sketched the first drawings of Mickey Mouse for Walt Disney and was Disney's business partner for many years. In a way, the two had grown up professionally together. Disney was a story man and the boss; Iwerks did the drawings. He was quick, with amazing skills in capturing Disney's story vision. A loyal member of Disney's team, Iwerks was rewarded with stock in Walt Disney Studios. Then, in a time of hardship for the struggling animation studio, Iwerks and other Disney artists were lured away by a competitor.

Walt Disney was devastated and probably felt betrayed. Iwerks had literally been his right-hand man. The split was ugly, causing hurt feelings and lots of stress, but Disney regrouped, hired new people, and continued to produce cartoons. Iwerks sold his stock shares back to Disney for a minuscule amount and went his own way.

Fast forward many years, and Walt Disney became incredibly successful. His films not only made lots of money at the box office, but they became beloved classics that changed moviemaking. Disney became known as *the* creative place to work, the place where quality was the order of the day.

But what happened to Ub Iwerks and the company that had lured him away? They are nearly forgotten to history. The company did not endure, and the cartoonist had to swallow his pride and go back to ask Disney for a job. Fortunately, the latter valued talent more than he valued his pride. He knew the creativity his former partner was capable of, and despite the disloyalty and hard feelings, he hired him back. However, things would never be the same. Iwerks was not made a partner, he never again held a close working relationship with his boss, and he didn't regain the massive amount of Disney stock he'd sold for a song so many years before. (It's estimated that had he held on to those original stocks, Iwerks would've been a billionaire at the time of his death.)[9]

---

9. Bob Thomas, *Walt Disney: An American Original* (Glendale, CA: Disney Editions, 1994).

Although he did not return to his former position, Iwerks still made a huge impact, not just at Disney but also in the world of feature animation. After returning to the studio, he moved into technical development and designed an optical printer for which he received an Academy Award. He ended up winning two Oscars in his lifetime and was inducted as a Disney Legend posthumously in 1989.[10]

It may not have been his original dream, but Ub Iwerks moved past his mistake, accepted the change, and ran with it, heavily contributing to the success of both Walt Disney Animation Studios and Disney theme parks.

We can't undo our decisions—and that is the first thing we need to accept in order for transformation to even begin to happen.

Forgiveness and restoration are important elements in repairing a relationship that has been broken or betrayed, but decisions sometimes have lasting consequences. We can't undo our decisions, however—and that is the first thing we need to accept in order for transformation to even begin to happen.

It's not about being able to undo the past. It's about how we take what we've learned and make something beautiful. That is how we commence on the road of un-failing.

Peter denied Christ but was then made whole through forgiveness and restoration. He could not undo what he did, but Peter could find greater devotion and greater love on the other side of failure. The remainder of Peter's life was a lesson learned and a continual lesson lived. But first he had to receive Jesus's forgiveness and restoration. These two incredibly freeing things allowed Peter to refocus and, eventually, jump-start his new ministry. Peter had to admit his failure, accept Jesus's forgiveness, and forgive himself. Then he was free to move on to a better place than where he

10. "Disney Legends: Ub Iwerks," *Walt Disney Archives*, d23.com/walt-disney-legend/ub-iwerks.

started, a wiser place. From then on, Peter would live with more intention and an even greater passion.

> *Forgiveness and redemption await even after our worst betrayals and mistakes.*

What a poignant reminder to each of us that forgiveness and redemption await even after our worst betrayals and mistakes. Jesus is not waiting to tell any of us, "I told you so, you were rotten." Christ is preparing invitations for all of us to leave the guilt and embarrassment and depression of our wrongs behind and instead to sit and eat with Him, to be made right. He is waiting for us to see that there is something better that can be made out of our failures, that we can keep moving forward, even if our lives feel drastically changed from what they were before. He prepared fish for Peter, but He has an endless store of healing food to prepare for us all. He has just what we need to be made whole.

SCRIPTURE TOOLS

The LORD has rewarded me according to my righteousness, according to my cleanness in his sight. (2 Samuel 22:25)

So [Naaman] went down and dipped himself in the Jordan seven times, as the man of God had told him, and his flesh was restored and became clean like that of a young boy. (2 Kings 5:14)

And when he prayed, the LORD listened to him and was moved by his request. So the LORD brought Manasseh back to Jerusalem and to his kingdom. Then Manasseh finally realized that the LORD alone is God! (2 Chronicles 33:13 NLT)

If you return to the Almighty, you will be restored: If you remove wickedness far from your tent.　　　　　　　　　　　　　(Job 22:23)

Once more Jesus put his hands on the man's eyes. Then his eyes were opened, his sight was restored, and he saw everything clearly.
　　　　　　　　　　　　　　　　　　　　　　　　(Mark 8:25)

I appeal to you, dear brothers and sisters, by the authority of our Lord Jesus Christ, to live in harmony with each other. Let there be no divisions in the church. Rather, be of one mind, united in thought and purpose.　　　　　　　　　　(1 Corinthians 1:10 NLT)

REFLECTION QUESTIONS

Here are some reflection questions you might consider when evaluating and developing a life of restoration:

3. Peter was a passionate follower of Christ. Passion can be emotional, and emotion can sometimes trip up even those with the best intentions. How do you think you would have fared if you had been questioned after the arrest of Christ? Why was Peter so emotional and scared in that moment?

4. What do you think Peter felt when the rooster crowed? Have you had similar moments when you've suddenly realized you've crossed certain lines and chosen not to stand with Christ? What did you feel in those moments? What are things you can do to keep close to Christ and avoid separation in the future?

5. Think of Jesus cooking on the seashore for Peter and the disciples. Has anyone you've wronged ever shown you such grace? How did you respond?

6. Have you ever been so loving to another, forgiving their wrongs and seeking them? What did you do to restore that relationship, and how can that help others?

7. Peter walked on the water with Christ, although briefly. In what ways are you stepping out of the boat to walk with Him? What scares you and causes you to go back to your seat rather than walking on the water with Christ? How can you overcome some of these fears to step out and stroll?

2

FACING THE TRUTH

(2 Samuel 11–12)

While some failures may be out of our control, others are the result of our own poor choices. And when the consequences start to build up, it can be highly tempting to hide what we've done or run as far away as possible. The thing is, when it comes down to it, this can happen to any of us, no matter how pious we felt before we fell or how long we'd been on a great and honest track with God. No one is above making a major mistake. None of us are above occasionally falling prey to our own desires and vulnerabilities.

But sin and its consequences don't just go away because we want them to, and when we attempt to cover them up, we may end up landing in a larger mess than we were in initially. One mistake leads to another, and then our failure has become something larger than we ever imagined.

> *Facing the truth might be the hardest thing we've ever done, but sometimes it's the only way forward.*

Facing the truth might be the hardest thing we've ever done, but sometimes it's the only way forward. God can still meet us in this place, but we have to be ready to be honest with ourselves.

THE STORY OF KING DAVID

A prime example that no one is invulnerable to bad decisions—no matter how well set up they seem—is King David. One of the most well-known characters in Scripture, David had such faith and trust in God, such integrity, and such a love for other people that he's even referred to in the Bible as "a man after God's own heart." (See 1 Samuel 13:14.)

David exhibited the traits of courage, ingenuity, faithfulness, and resolve early on as a shepherd boy. He had guts, boldness—no one could refute that. In the story of Goliath, David wasn't about to let anyone talk smack against his people or his God, even this Philistine giant who terrorized the Israelites. It didn't matter that David was simply a boy. He stood up even when the king, Saul, was unable or unwilling to do so.

It didn't dawn on David that he might not be capable. His faith led to Goliath's defeat, and his trust in God remained even when King Saul threatened his life in return. David remained humble when victorious in battle, and throughout all of it, he kept his eyes on God, giving Him the glory. Because of this, God blessed him. Not only did he become king, but God promised David victory over his enemies and told him his descendants would rule over God's people forever. At this point, David's life looks like the epitome of success.

Still, all of this didn't make David perfect. Yes, he was absolutely set up to succeed, but at the pinnacle of his success, he made a mistake that would determine the course and the quality of the rest of his life. Because here is the thing about mistakes: you can't go back once you've made them. As much as we may want to, we can't change what we've already done. We can, however, allow those mistakes to change us for the better, instead of pushing us deeper into a hole.

Years after David was crowned king and was essentially at the top of his world, we find him in the middle of war. But things are different now. The brave boy we saw square off against Goliath is no longer around. The whole Israelite army was sent to battle, minus David. He stayed home in Jerusalem. He didn't march off with his men; he sat around on his throne literally looking for trouble. And he found it.

One evening, David got up and walked along the roof of his palace. But he wasn't out there looking at the clouds or enjoying the sunset. No, he was watching a beautiful woman taking a bath. He was so taken by this lovely sight that he sent someone to find out about her. When his spy returned and reported, "She is Bathsheba, and she is married to Uriah the Hittite," David didn't balk; he sent men to retrieve her. They brought her to the king, David slept with her, and she became pregnant.

> *When Bathsheba became pregnant, David understood that immediate action was required—leading to his next mistake.*

Now, King David was no dummy. He knew he had a problem. First, he had sex with another man's wife. That was bad in and of itself, and David certainly knew it was wrong. Second, Bathsheba was now expecting his child. David understood that immediate action was required—leading to his next mistake. He formulated a plan and sent a messenger to the army, asking Uriah to report to him. Upon his arrival, David greeted Uriah and pretended to question him about how the men were progressing in the war, but it wasn't long before he slyly suggested that Uriah have a conjugal visit with his wife, saying, *"Go on home and relax"* (2 Samuel 11:8 NLT).

What David did not count on was Uriah's character. Perhaps years of being the king had changed David's perspective. He didn't remember what it was like to truly place himself in another's situation. But Uriah thought of his fellow soldiers, currently camped out in open country. He refused to go home to eat, drink, and make love to his wife. He told his king, "*I will not do such a thing!*" (2 Samuel 11:11).

This perplexed David. Uriah was messing with his plan. If Uriah didn't make love with Bathsheba, David's indiscretions would be discovered. So, David kept trying. He kept Uriah in Jerusalem another night to wine and dine him until Uriah was tipsy. But again, even with alcohol lowering his guard, Uriah would not go home; he slept on a mat among the king's servants.

David had endured enough. He lost his temper and wrote a note to Uriah's commander, Joab: "Put this soldier out front in the thick of the action. Then pull your troops back from him so that he will be struck down and killed."

It happened just as David requested. Joab placed Uriah in the front lines where the battle was fiercest, and Uriah the Hittite died.

David must have been pleased with himself. Just think about it! This man who used to be known for his integrity ensured the death of another man to hide his own transgression. Bathsheba mourned for her husband when she heard the news—but that didn't stop David from continuing to make plans. When the time of Bathsheba's mourning was over, David brought her to the palace and made her one of his wives. She later bore him a son.

At first, it seemed as though everything may have worked out for David, as if he'd gotten away with it all. But 2 Samuel 11:27 tells us, "*The thing David had done displeased the LORD.*" And God did something pretty interesting: He sent the prophet Nathan to rebuke David.

Nathan was a smart, experienced prophet. He knew the king and had prophesied many times in court. In lieu of barging in and throwing around allegations, Nathan instead chose to tell David a story about a rich man and a poor man. In the story, the rich man had everything while the poor man had nothing but a little lamb. The poor man raised the lamb, shared his food with it, and loved the lamb as if it were his child.

Nathan then told David that the rich man took the lamb from the poor man and ate it.

As he listened to the story, David became furious. He told the prophet, *"As surely as the LORD lives, the man who did this must die!"* (2 Samuel 12:5).

Nathan shouted at the king, *"You are that man!"*

In understanding Nathan's allegory about the rich man who ate the poor man's beloved lamb, David understood just how horribly he had sinned.

He reminded David that the Lord had appointed him king over Israel, had delivered him from the hand of Saul, and had given him wealth, power, and wives. He said God would have given David even more had he asked. But Nathan didn't stop there. He delivered a message from God: calamity would befall David and his house. God was going to punish David for the evil he'd committed.

At that point, David stopped Nathan, crying, *"I have sinned against the LORD"* (2 Samuel 12:13). Truly remorseful, he repented, and the Bible says that God heard him.

Nathan relayed a new message: *"The LORD has taken away your sin. You are not going to die."*

The relief David must have felt! Isn't that just like God? In moments when we deserve punishment, God often delivers grace. But unfortunately for David, that wasn't the end of the story. There are consequences to turning away from God. And David was about to find out how far-reaching those consequences can be. Even through forgiveness and repentance, there are repercussions when we make bad choices, and the king was not exempt from this reality. Nathan had brought David to his knees with his revelation, "You are that man!" There was forgiveness and restoration, but David had already opened the wrong door onto a new path.

GOD'S BLESSINGS REMOVED

First, because David had shown contempt to the Lord, Nathan reported that the son who was born to Bathsheba would die.

This is hard for us to understand. David pleaded with God for the life of the child—and we are on his side, pleading with him!—but it was not meant to be. The child became ill and on the seventh day, he passed away.

Then, from that point forward, God removed His hand from David's life. The rewarding life that David had lived before with God's easy blessings would be no more.

+ David's family lived by the sword.

+ His household rebelled against him.

+ His wives slept with another man—David's son, Absalom—in public, on the palace rooftop where David had spied on Bathsheba. (See 2 Samuel 16:21–22.) In other words, what David did in secret happened openly in the sight of all Israel.

Every aspect of David's life was transformed by his choices. He was able to put things back together in some way, but the repercussions of his sinful choices were never fully undone. David's family lived and died by the way sin dominated and defined David's life.

This story is especially tragic and frustrating when you recognize that God had poured His blessings on top of David in quarts and gallons, not pints. His was truly a story of amazing significance, amazing success. He had everything going for him. Then he messed up. He made some bad decisions: spying on Bathsheba, coveting her, and taking her. Here was a man after God's own heart who used his power over one of his subjects like she was a commodity. Here was a king who sought the death of one of his most loyal soldiers. One sin had led to another. David was not just an adulterer; he was a murderer.

Then it got worse. After Uriah's death, David tried to go back to his life as though nothing had happened. He had failed and, like many political leaders, his first thought was containment. *How do I control the story? How do I make this go away?* A posture of service to the King of heaven would be one of repentance and honesty, vulnerability and brokenness. That approach would have been a strong witness; God could have used

David's sin for His glory. But instead, David tried to cover it all up, push it away, and forget it ever happened.

At every turn, David's plans for damage control fell apart and led to something worse. For a king, this would be quite difficult to stomach—everything is on display, everything can undermine how your people see you, and there are higher stakes. David was accustomed to having things go his way, but he forgot a crucial truth: we cannot control or contain our sin.

> *Sin is slimy, too able to go around the edges of our lives. We cannot compartmentalize it and expect it to stay put.*

Sin is too big for us. It's too slimy, too able to flow around the edges of our lives. We cannot compartmentalize it and expect it to stay put.

When we sin, regardless of how small or large it is, or how much we believe we can slide it under the rug with ease, it has the potential to slide back out.

A MILLION LOOSE MARBLES

On a trip to Washington, DC, we took a riverboat cruise down the Potomac to Mount Vernon. A family was playing marbles in a section of the boat with tables set up for games. As the boat shifted in the current, the couple's young son scurried off, trying to catch the marbles as they scattered everywhere. Over and over, the boat would rock, and the boy would try to capture the loose marbles.

Up to that point, we hadn't really thought about how much the boat was moving. We were relatively unaffected by the motion. But once those marbles started rolling around, the boat's movement was unavoidably evident. No matter what he did, the boy was unable to keep the marbles in place because everything around him was rocking, even when he didn't realize it.

Our lives are constantly rocking. They shift back and forth, and there's a lot going on that maybe we can't see until we try to keep everything in place. David's pieces were all over the place, so he moved from containment to cover-up—and that's when things became very serious. David made one decision that led to another … and another … and another … until finally, an innocent man, Uriah, was dead.

> *Sin puts everything in jeopardy—our relationships, our word, and our kinship with God—and David's fall demonstrates this.*

When sin has invaded our life, containment isn't possible, even if we don't realize it yet. Sin puts everything in jeopardy—our relationships, our word, and our kinship with God—and the story of David's fall demonstrates this. When we indulge in this kind of behavior, making choices that we know aren't right, we're releasing marbles in many directions. Trying to catch them all ourselves instead of turning to God can lead down a road of deeper mistakes, pushing us even further from Him.

You cannot undo the damage that sin causes. David could not resurrect Uriah nor could he erase his night with Bathsheba. The moment he made that first decision to sleep with Bathsheba, the marbles were already spreading out in every direction. Trying to contain them just scattered them farther.

We always have choices. We might be dealing with some tough things, it might be embarrassing or feel like it's the end of the world to recognize our failure and own up to our mistakes, but we can always choose good over evil. When we choose to cover up, we choose evil. But we still can't outrun the truth.

In the Watergate scandal in the early 1970s, President Nixon did not order the burglars to break into the Democratic National Committee headquarters. He did not plan the operation. In fact, when he heard about it, he was surprised and angry. Nixon's sin was that when he found out about it, he lied. It was the cover-up that did him in.

Fear of the truth coming out brought down the president of the United States. The same fear brought down David, the greatest king that Israel has ever known.

WE ARE NOT THE EXCEPTION

Several years ago, a local newspaper had an article about raccoons. It reported that although raccoons can be quite cute as pets when they are young, a significant problem arises later. Somewhere between the ages of twenty-four to thirty months, raccoons go through a glandular change and become incredibly aggressive and dangerous.

The reporter had a friend who owned a young pet raccoon. After doing some research for his story, he called his friend and said, "I've come across some very important raccoon information for you."

He asked about the raccoon's age and was told that it was about eighteen to nineteen months old. He warned his friend about the glandular change that occurs in raccoons around age two. He cautioned her that her pet was likely to become aggressive and suggested that she bring the pet to a shelter. Tragically, the woman did not believe her friend. She believed she could handle her beloved pet. She believed *her* raccoon was different.

Toward the end of his article, the reporter sadly notes that his friend required reconstructive plastic surgery on her face because the raccoon eventually attacked her. It turns out raccoons have incredible strength; their bite is comparable to that of an angry, one-hundred-pound dog.

We all tend to believe we've got things under control.
We assume we can handle this temptation or
that stumbling block.

Much like this woman who thought she'd be fine and normal raccoon behavior didn't necessarily apply to her own situation, we all tend to believe we've got things under control. We assume we can handle this temptation or that stumbling block. That we can manage the relationship at work that is leading us down a dodgy path or the lie we've told that keeps getting worse. We think we can be a little bit dishonest, a little bit shady with our finances, that we can indulge in a tiny bit of dishonesty with our work and our teams. We assume things will be fine. We can handle it; we've got it.

Friends, those are the famous last words before the adversary pounces on our lives. That is us refusing to face the truth. If a man after God's own heart could not handle sin, neither can we. We are not different. We are not special. We are just as able to succumb to temptation and sin as anyone else.

And by the time we get to the end of that road of running and lying and covering our tracks, aren't we tired? When we encounter that dead end that comes with avoiding the truth, we don't want a Nathan in our lives, rebuking us for where we find ourselves. We don't want to hear it, but sometimes it's exactly what we need to hear to actually face up to the truth of our lives.

There was a preacher friend of ours who preached a lot on sin. After sharing a three-week series on sin at his church, a laity leader came to see him. The leader said, "You know what? We wish you wouldn't preach on sin so much. It really is hurting our attendance. If you can just kind of tone it down a little bit, maybe things will be better."

Our friend told the lay leader that he had a bottle of strychnine on one of his shelves. He said, "Well, why don't we do this. Why don't I just take off this label that says 'Poison: Strychnine,' and I'll put a cane syrup label on it, and we'll just have everybody drink it." The laity leader said that was the stupidest thing he'd ever heard. Our friend said, "Well, what you just said to me may rival it."

The milder we make the label, the more potent we make the poison.

We must be ready to both face each other with the truth and accept the truth. Watering it down doesn't do us any good. If anything, it makes us think we'll be okay when we won't be. We need more Nathans sharing wisdom and truth in love. We need to *be* Nathans for those we love. And we need to recognize that we are not the exception. We won't be able to cover up or contain what we've done.

FINDING GRACE FOR OURSELVES

David realized too late how great the costs would be. There are major repercussions when our sin gets the best of us. Not only did the cost apply to Uriah, but there was also the cost to Bathsheba and her child, the cost of David's reputation, and the cost to David's descendants, who fought among themselves for generations.

When all was said and done, David could learn to forgive himself and accept God's forgiveness, but moving past his sin was an entirely different matter. Although our forgiveness is based in God's grace, reminders of our failures will always be pushed and prodded and beaten down on us by the adversary.

Satan wants you to remember your worst. Though you may have forgiven another or received forgiveness for what's happened in your life, if the adversary can whisper one more negative thought, if he can put one more dangerous word in your mind, then maybe he can keep you right where he wants you. Sin doesn't just eat away at the emotional side of us; it eats away at the spiritual side too.

Finding grace for ourselves when we've messed up can be a struggle, but the alternative of hopelessness and giving up is not God's plan for us. Facing ourselves, facing the truth, can be hard, but we are not alone. We must remember this.

One of the most heart-wrenching photographs ever shot shows a vulture and a starving little boy in the Sudan. The image was taken in 1993 by Kevin Carter, a photojournalist. It shows an emaciated young child slumped over in the foreground, back exposed and ribs sticking out. (The child was initially thought to be a girl, perhaps because he was wearing a necklace and bracelets.)[11] The boy had stopped on his way to a United Nations feeding station; his parents had gone on ahead to collect food. A vulture had landed behind the boy and was inching closer, waiting for him to die.

Carter had to approach the subject very carefully. When the vulture got close enough to be in focus with the child, Carter took a few photos before chasing it away.

---

11. Alberto Rojas, "Kong Nyong, el niño que sobrevivió al buitre (Kong Nyong, the boy who survived the vulture)," El Mundo, February 21, 2011, www.elmundo.es/elmundo/2011/02/18/comunicacion/1298054483.html.

But that was all he did. He did not carry the boy to the feeding center. He did not do anything further to assist this weak child in need. He'd taken his photos, so he left.

The New York Times was the first to publish the photo. It immediately caused great controversy. Hundreds of people called the newspaper to see if the child had survived. The *Times* had no answer; they didn't know the child's fate. People condemned Carter for not helping the child, even though photojournalists in the region had been warned not to touch famine victims for fear of spreading disease to them. The *St. Petersburg Times* commented: "The man adjusting his lens to take just the right frame of her suffering might just as well be a predator, another vulture on the scene."

A few months after receiving the 1994 Pulitzer Prize for Feature Photography for his photo, Kevin Carter died by suicide at the age of thirty-three. He left behind a note that read in part: "I'm really, really sorry. The pain of life overrides the joy to the point that joy does not exist."[12]

There probably was little Carter could have done to change the long-term situation for that boy. Many kids were dying daily in Sudan; his situation was not unique. That reality, though, was not enough for Carter to rationalize his inaction to himself. For him, the truth was still too hard. By not doing enough, in his mind, and despite receiving great reward afterward for his photograph, it was just all too much for the depressed photographer to handle. Instead of asking forgiveness and trying to move forward, like King David, the photographer saw no way for redemption; he felt no possibility of escape.

From our failure, we can experience forgiveness. We can move forward without being eternally weighed down by guilt.

The child's situation was tragic, but there is also great sadness in reflecting upon the depression and suicide of the young photojournalist.

---

12. Scott Macleod, "The Life and Death of Kevin Carter," *Time Magazine*, September 12, 1994, content.time.com/time/subscriber/article/0,33009,981431,00.html.

God offers forgiveness, redemption, and restoration to those who seek Him. He will help collect the scattered marbles, hold us steady as we face the truth of our actions, and offer us grace to move forward. Just as David found favor by offering a humble heart and Peter was redeemed by Jesus, we can also find grace in those times when we've been our worst selves. From our failure, we can experience forgiveness and a better perspective on life. We can move forward without being eternally weighed down by guilt. This is the freedom that Jesus wants us to live in.

ACCEPTING THE TRUTH

There is hope when we've failed and find ourselves in unwanted circumstances. Repentance and forgiveness can lead us to a whole new experience of wholeness. On the other side of failure, our relationships can be restored. Brokenness can lead to unity. We can be lifted up with grace and forgiveness and redemption. We can face the truth. When we turn back and admit that we made a mistake, although the repercussions may follow us, we open new doors with God by our side.

Even through the tragedy of losing his son and taking away his many blessings, God had not forgotten David. He and Bathsheba had another son, Solomon, who was an ancestor of Jesus's foster father, Joseph, while their son Nathan was an ancestor of Jesus's mother Mary. Through weak and fragile people, God would provide the salvation of the world. Through the blood of those who failed, God would bring the blood of the One who would succeed eternally. Through God, David would embark on a journey of un-failing, of living in recognition of what he'd done without being consumed by it. And God's promises would still hold fast.

As we seek restoration, there is hope. Even if we feel we're in a dark place, pinned by our former choices and where they've led, there is hope. Maybe you're in the midst of one of those dark places. Maybe you're running from sin or trying to cover it up. We want to invite you to give those sins over to the Lord. Don't continue to try to navigate and control and contain and cover up—because you can't do it. The only thing that you can do is to turn it all over to the Lord and say, "I don't want to live behind the secrets any longer." All we can do is accept the truth: that we will all fail again and again and we all need to continue handing our lives over to God.

In the midst of all of it, we want you to know something. Please know that you are indeed loved. We want you to hear the words of the Lord, said to David through the prophet Nathan: "If you had just come to Me and told Me what you were dealing with, I would have met you in that place."

The Lord wants to meet you in that place.

SCRIPTURE TOOLS

Your sins are telling your mouth what to say. Your words are based on clever deception. (Job 15:5 NLT)

These are the things that you shall do: Speak the truth to one another; render in your gates judgments that are true and make for peace. (Zechariah 8:16 ESV)

When he, the Spirit of truth, comes, he will guide you into all the truth. He will not speak on his own; he will speak only what he hears, and he will tell you what is yet to come. (John 16:13)

We will speak the truth in love, growing in every way more and more like Christ. (Ephesians 4:15 NLT)

The man who saw it has given testimony, and his testimony is true. He knows that he tells the truth, and he testifies so that you also may believe. (John 19:35)

You rebuke the arrogant, who are accursed, those who stray from your commands. (Psalm 119:21)

A rebuke goes deeper into a man of understanding than a hundred blows into a fool. (Proverbs 17:10 ESV)

REFLECTION QUESTIONS

Here are some reflection questions you might consider when evaluating and developing a life of openness to the truth spoken in love:

1. David got in trouble when he became bored with his life of luxury and riches. He had everything yet wanted more. What dangers do we face in our own lavish lives in today's world? Could it be that sometimes less really can be more?

2. It's been suggested by some biblical scholars that David had seen Bathsheba before, that he had returned again and again, and the choice he made was not a spur-of-the-moment decision. Are there ways to safeguard ourselves by avoiding temptation in our own lives? Does this approach perhaps require different choices in our viewing habits for television, the Internet, and other media? What are ways we can protect ourselves from ourselves?

3. Uriah was faithful to his men and his position. He did not seek his own comforts. This makes David's sins against Uriah all the more tragic. How many chances was David given through this scenario to do the right thing, to change course? It started with one sin that snowballed into greater sins. How does this speak to our own walks and decisions?

4. Everyone needs a Nathan in their lives. Is it easy to hear someone speak truth to us? Does it make it easier if that person loves us? For whom are you being called to be a Nathan?

5. David did repent and found favor again with the Lord. The other side of failure for David was a restored walk with God. What mistakes have you made that taught you about the heart of God after repentance and restoration?

3

BLOOMING WHERE
WE'RE PLANTED

(Jonah 1–4)

Regardless of our position in society, we only get to choose our lives to a certain degree. Some aspects of life will remain perpetually out our hands, leaving us without the ability to change our circumstances. We can only control how we respond to them.

Sometimes, this means we end up in situations we never would have chosen for ourselves. As much as we may want to rail against the circumstances, our only option is to make the best decisions we can while dealing with them. This can mean accepting that our lives are part of a larger story. It can also mean accepting that what God is asking of us may not be what we wanted for ourselves. But when God is asking us to make the best of a hard situation, what are we choosing to do? Sulk? Yell at Him? Run away?

Our mistakes may land us in situations we don't want to be in, but God can use those situations too. Just because we're in hot water doesn't mean God is absent. We need to open our eyes and hearts to what God is making possible through our mistakes, how He's using the results of our shortcomings to create change in the world around us or through us.

Whether our failure led us into our circumstances or made them ten times worse than they could have been, we do have options. We have the ability to un-fail, to use what we have to make something better. We can choose to make the most of wherever we are, however we ended up there, whatever the conditions.

THE STORY OF JONAH

Jonah did not like the situation he was given. God commanded him to travel northeast to the big city of Nineveh and preach against it, but Jonah decided to say no to God. He didn't want to help the pagans, who were Israel's enemies, so he hopped on a ship destined for Tarshish in the opposite direction.

Imagine Jonah's surprise when the Lord sent a harsh windstorm to upset the boat he was on. Violent waves slammed against it, and everyone on board was terrified. There were plenty of prayers and screams heard amidst the howling wind, as the crew frantically threw the cargo into the sea to keep the vessel from sinking. Even so, it seemed the ship would go down.

Jonah was not among the frantic men on deck. He had gone below and fallen into a deep sleep. The captain was furious when he saw his sleeping passenger. As the raging sea continued to batter the boat, the captain shook Jonah awake, yelling, "How can you sleep at a time like this? Get up, call on your God, and ask Him to spare us!"

Meanwhile, the sailors were taking matters into their own hands. They cast lots to see who was responsible for this disaster. Of course, the lot fell on Jonah.

"Who are you?!" the sailors cried. "What did you do? Where are you from? Why is this happening to us?" Probably not without great reservations, Jonah told them the truth: he worshipped the Lord who made the land and the seas, and he was running from his God.

This frightened the sailors even more. The sea became more tumultuous, and it seemed like the waves would sink the ship at any second. The panic reached a fevered pitch, and the crew cried out, "What can we do to make this stop?!"

It must have been difficult for Jonah to say it, but he answered, "Throw me overboard, and the storm will cease. It's my fault this is happening."

To their credit, the crew didn't immediately toss Jonah overboard. They tried to row back to land, but *the sea grew even wilder than before* (Jonah 1:13). They hated to do it, but the men finally grabbed Jonah, said a prayer asking God for forgiveness, and tossed him into the raging waters.

The sea immediately became calm. On the surface, it was a stark contrast to the tribulation everyone had been facing only moments before. But now the crew greatly feared God. In the water, Jonah had plenty of his own fears beyond being submerged and possibly drowning. A huge fish swam by, opened its mouth, and swallowed Jonah whole. He spent three long days and three long nights in its belly.

In the belly of the great fish, Jonah had time to mull over all of his missteps, pray, and reconsider his actions.

That would be quite the predicament. It would certainly be a time of reflection and soul-searching, swaying back and forth in the strange, smelly darkness, mulling over all the missteps that led him there. It gave Jonah the time and space he needed to reconsider his actions. Jonah spent a lot of time in prayer. "You hurled me into the sea, Lord, and I've been barred from Your sight. But You heard my prayer, Lord." He asked forgiveness and repented of running away from God's command. "I'll go," Jonah said. "I'll tell Ninevah that salvation comes from the Lord."

At this, God commanded the fish to vomit Jonah up onto dry land. The Lord said again, "Go to Nineveh and give them My message." This time, Jonah obeyed.

It would not be an easy task. Nineveh was a huge city. It would be daunting to be the lone messenger of the Lord, denouncing the city's wicked ways. But Jonah proclaimed the warning: in forty days, Nineveh would be overthrown. (See Jonah 3:4.)

You might think that this crazy man appearing with his predictions of doom and gloom would be too much for the Ninevites to swallow (pardon the pun), but an amazing thing happened. The Ninevites believed him! The king declared that everyone in the city should fast and be covered with sackcloth, pray to God, and give up their wicked ways. The king reasoned, *"Who knows? God may yet relent and with compassion turn from his fierce anger so that we will not perish"* (Jonah 3:9).

And that's just what happened. God saw their repentance and relented, pleased at the conversion of Nineveh. It's likely that the entire city celebrated.

Everyone except Jonah.

Jonah was ticked off. He did not like these people. He railed to God, "I knew You weren't going to kill them! I knew You'd be compassionate to them! Just kill me now!" Jonah was angry that God had forgiven them. *"But the LORD replied, 'Is it right for you to be angry?'"* (Jonah 4:4).

But Jonah wasn't listening. He stormed off like a petulant child, went out of the city, built a shelter, and waited to see what else would happen to Nineveh. He was pouting. This had not gone at all like he had hoped. He wanted no part of it.

The sun rose, and the Lord grew a plant to give Jonah shade. But as the sun still blazed overhead, God sent a worm to eat the plant, which shriveled, and Jonah grew faint from the heat. He moaned again, complaining, "I'm better off dead!"

"But God said to Jonah, 'Is it right for you to be angry about the plant?'" (Jonah 4:9).

"Yes, indeed!" said Jonah. "I'm so angry that I wish I were dead!"

The Lord then chastised Jonah. "Here you are worried about this plant that you didn't tend. The plant just grew and died. You're concerned about it and not the souls of a city full of people." God explained:

Should I not have concern for the great city of Nineveh, in which there are more than a hundred and twenty thousand people who cannot tell their right hand from their left—and also many animals?

(Jonah 4:11)

Jonah thought the plant God grew for him shouldn't have died because it was convenient for him and helped him. But the people of Nineveh—an entire city of living, breathing human beings who had lived in sin and then repented—didn't deserve God's grace. The reluctant prophet found no joy in their salvation. How dare the city actually listen to Jonah's words and change its ways? How dare God use him to help people he didn't like, people he didn't want to help?

GETTING PAST OURSELVES

We may not like God's plan. We may not like what God asks us to do. We may find ourselves upset at the circumstances we find ourselves in—they weren't what we thought they would be. We may end up helping to change lives or offering God's grace to people we don't particularly care for. However, this life is about more than just us. For us to refuse to try is a mistake. To just pout and be angry about it is a waste of our time.

The *big reveal* of the Bible is that *"God is love"* (1 John 4:16). Jonah's big problem was that he had no love for the people of Nineveh. He took a three-day detour to avoid even talking to them. Even after God showed amazing grace to the inhabitants of the city, Jonah still could not get past his hatred.

Loving those we disagree with can be difficult.
It requires getting past our prejudices, feelings, and hurts.

Loving those we disagree with can be difficult. It requires getting past our prejudices, feelings, and hurts, getting past those tapes playing in our head telling us that some people are not good enough, not worthy enough of help. "You want me to minister to whom?" we ask. "You want me to lead them?!"

It takes getting past ourselves. Blooming where we're planted, even if it's not what we expected, even if it's not exactly what we want.

MORE THAN JUST US

We love the movie *Sister Act*, starring Whoopi Goldberg.[13] It's a fun musical, and it reminds us of the story of Jonah. Goldberg's character, Deloris, is also sent somewhere she doesn't wish to go.

A casino lounge singer, Deloris witnesses a murder and is sent into witness protection at a convent. Deloris is asked to earn her room and board by helping the enthusiastic but undisciplined choir of nuns. Naturally, the movie has a Hollywood ending: the choir is transformed by Deloris's efforts into an amazing ensemble that ultimately sings for the pope. Through all the adversity, Deloris comes to realize that she had a greater purpose and was placed with the nuns for a reason.

Sister Act really gives a pretty common picture of how God works. In our lives, we often find ourselves in jobs, positions, or roles where we are uncomfortable. Like Deloris in the movie, we can think only of removing ourselves from that situation. We try to get free rather than remain in the struggle. We fail to remember that this is how God teaches us lessons or skills that we will need further along in our journey. The old adage says, "Bloom where you are planted." There is wisdom in this. Of course, this is not to say that we are to give up or become hopeless when life seems stagnant. It means that instead of only trying to find a way of escape, we should also strive to learn lessons and gain insight through our struggle.

We should strive to learn lessons and gain insight when we find ourselves in uncomfortable situations.

---

13. *Sister Act*, directed by Emile Ardolino (1992; Buena Vista Pictures Distribution).

Another aspect we love about this particular film is that Deloris eventually learns to help others even though she was resistant at first. Deloris didn't want to help the lackluster choir. She was used to belting out show tunes and Motown music to rowdy audiences. The choir's hymns were simply not her style. It was only when Deloris took the sentiment from the choir's repertoire and fused that with the feel of her own music that she discovered she had something to offer that was worthy of the effort. The choir took the melody of "My Guy" and made it work for church services by rewriting the lyrics to say, "My God."

Had Deloris simply left the protection of the convent, she would've missed out on many things. She would not have forged the many new friendships that she ultimately treasured. She wouldn't have discovered important leadership qualities she already possessed but didn't fully appreciate. She wouldn't have found a whole new genre of music to explore. She wouldn't have had the opportunity to help other people so directly. She definitely wouldn't have seen so much personal growth if she had remained just another lounge singer. And, last but not least, Deloris's gangster boyfriend might have had her killed had she left the convent walls! There were definite benefits to remaining right where she was planted.

Blooming where God placed her benefited other people too. By giving of her talents and her large personality, not only did the nuns in the choir loosen up and sing much better but the entire neighborhood found new life. The engaging music brought people into the failing church. The nuns reached out with new gusto, refurbishing the surrounding areas and engaging their neighbors with good news. The change in Deloris's attitude greatly affected everyone around her. There was a greater good at play than just one woman's transformation. As Deloris grew and matured, as she accepted and embraced her tasks, as she un-failed from her former life and attitude, the whole world of the convent—indeed, the whole neighborhood—benefited.

This is just like God. Because it wasn't just about Deloris; our lives affect others too. His perfect plan works for the good of everyone if we choose to let go and let God work. Sometimes God allows us to struggle in our situations so we can have the greatest impact.

How often do we grumble and complain rather than find what needs to be done to make the world better? The tragedy is that so many people willfully choose to simply not bloom. They fail to act, to grow. They remain planted, but there is no joy, no expression of beauty, no life. Like Jonah, they rail against what they don't like, try to run from their problems, and refuse to let their situation teach them anything new.

After Hurricane Katrina, the Mississippi Annual Conference of the United Methodist Church started to use a wonderful image featuring a bright green sprig of new growth popping up through a concrete slab left by the storm's destruction. This vibrant image is a great reminder for each of us. If we find ourselves in an undesirable position at work, in a relationship, or in life, the best thing to do is the best job we can. Our faithfulness and determination can be the agent of change, not only for ourselves, but for our entire world.

FOR THE GOOD OF THE TEAM

Accepting where we are and blooming where we're planted requires getting out of our own heads, thinking beyond our own needs, and remembering that our lives are part of something larger. We are always going to be rubbing elbows with other people, for better or worse. We can huddle in our own world and focus only on what we want, *or* we can bloom with what we have and recognize that we are not alone and this world works better when we're part of it. God may have plans for us that are more about the good of everyone than what's beneficial specifically for us.

> *God may have plans for us that are more about the good of everyone than what's beneficial specifically for us.*

Being part of God's plan is kind of like being involved in a team sport. It works best when everyone puts aside their own issues and works strictly for the good of the team. When the coach calls a play, it doesn't work if the players decide to run in the opposite direction, but that's exactly what

Jonah did. He tried playing his own game, and God wasn't having it. Jonah wasn't coachable; he wasn't a good teammate.

We do the same thing today. We say no to God. We do this more often than we can possibly imagine. How many opportunities to do good are placed in front of us on a daily basis? God gives us chances to participate with Him, to be a part of His kingdom work. And it is oh so easy for us to turn a deaf ear. Our prejudices, insecurities, and fears sometimes keep us from the fullness of participation. Using the analogy of a football game, God creates play after play in which He tries to hand us the ball so we can run with it. We've known lots of athletes who talk about the rush they feel when they're in the zone. It's adrenaline. It's accomplishment. It's a buzz that those of us who wait on the sidelines never get to feel. But participation requires being coachable, recognizing that we're part of a team. It takes effort and a certain selflessness to keep responding to those commands, accepting the input, and putting it into action.

We are created for communion with the God of the universe. He wants to speak to us. Sometimes it comes in whispers from the Holy Spirit. Those are the quiet nudges where we feel the call to action, where God tries to give us guidance toward something good for us. Often, we ignore these whispers, choosing instead to chart our own course. Imagine the incredible works we've chosen not to accomplish when we ignore the nudges of the Spirit.

Sometimes God calls the play a little louder. The directions are clearer when this happens. Often, we hear someone say, "God was trying to get my attention." It is harder to ignore the thunder when we hear it, and yet sometimes we do. Like Jonah, we still try to run the other way. We try to hide from the decision or the path that is clearly before us, even as the winds and seas start to rage.

Sometimes our piety gets the better of us. We want to continue our judging, or we slip into some kind of default that shouts, "I've got it figured out, and God must love me best cause I'm following Him!"

Being a Christ follower requires mercy, forgiveness, patience, kindness, and listening. It requires forgetting about ourselves and giving ourselves up for the good of the team, doing the best we can, exactly where we are. That is how we begin to walk on the path to un-failing, to making our lives what they were meant to be.

KEEP DOING THE WORK

Singer/songwriter Bill Gaither grew up on a family farm in Alexandria, Indiana. He listened to the Statesmen Quartet harmonizing on the old barn radio each morning before school as he milked the cows. Young Bill dreamed of nothing more than traveling with a famous Southern gospel quartet, singing and playing toe-tapping music. He learned to play the piano and sang heartily with his brother and sister all over the area. Then, one day, the college freshman got a phone call that thrilled him to the core: the famous Weatherford Quartet wanted Bill to join their group as a piano player. The moment had come. Bill was to have his dream fulfilled and ride off into the sunset as a Southern gospel quartet member.

It never happened.

When the excited young man shared the great news with his father, Bill's dad told him he didn't want his son to quit college. He told Bill to finish school, then he could pursue music.

Bill was heartbroken. Being an obedient son, he would not go against his father's wishes, so he remained in school and watched as another pianist took his place. Bill finished his degree in English, then taught high school and met another young teacher named Gloria. The two dated, married, and began to write songs together. Though Bill gave up hope of being in a great quartet, he still wanted to contribute to the kingdom of God through songwriting. He and Gloria went on to pen some great Christian anthems like "Because He Lives," "The King Is Coming," "Something Beautiful," and "The Family of God." The Bill Gaither Trio went on to become the most successful contemporary Christian group of its time. In fact, Bill is considered a father of modern contemporary Christian music. He took the gospel into all sorts of new places and sold millions of albums. For years and years, God blessed Bill and his endeavors. Bill had been faithful to both his father and his calling, and the blessings poured on the Gaithers. But it still wasn't the music that Bill Gaither loved the most.

Toward the late 1980s, album sales began to dwindle. People weren't attending the Bill Gaither Trio concerts as they once had. Bill was tired and decided it was time to retire and let younger people have the stage. But before then, he decided to record one more album just for himself. He knew it wouldn't be a big seller, but it was something he wanted to do. He would record an album of old Southern gospel classics and call it *Homecoming*.

However, the album did sell—quite well, in fact. And at the very moment Bill was thinking his career was over, God was revealing to Bill that another one, the career he had always wanted, was waiting just around the corner. It was as if God said, "No, no, son. You've been faithful in these things all these years, and now I've got a surprise for you!"

The Gaither Vocal Band became the best known and best loved group in the industry. Bill is now known as the king of Southern gospel music. The *Gaither Homecoming* videos have sold millions of copies around the world, and the concert tours have sold more than a million tickets around the world, comparable to rock and country music acts. You can't flip through the television channels at night without coming across Gaither programming. The Southern gospel style is now nearly synonymous with Bill Gaither. The world—and television—has never been the same.[14]

Even when we think our dreams are lost, a life of character and hard work often leads to the things we desire most.

It's a beautiful reminder that obedience to God often pays off in unexpected ways. We realize that even when we think our dreams are lost, a life of character and hard work often leads to the things we desire most. We have not failed simply because we haven't seen our dreams come true yet. We just need to keep doing the work with what we have. And then, when we think we've gotten everything out of life that we will receive, God opens

14. Bill Gaither, *I Almost Missed the Sunset: My Perspectives on Life and Music* (Nashville, TN: Thomas Nelson, 1992).

a storehouse to share His goodness with those He loves. God works in mysterious ways. Sometimes we must lose it all to find everything.

THE CHOICE IS OURS

Whether our own choices or powers beyond our control land us in a less-than-ideal spot, we need to hold on and use what we do have. Even if it feels like failure to be stuck or waiting or not achieving our dreams yet, we have the opportunity to turn our situation into an un-fail. God used Jonah even when Jonah couldn't see past himself. Jonah helped to save an entire city by simply saying yes to God. We can't run from God or what life has in store for us, but we can choose to look at it in a new light. We can choose to bloom wherever we find ourselves planted. We can choose to un-fail, accept our role on the team, and keep doing the work, no matter what God asks of us.

SCRIPTURE TOOLS

Serve wholeheartedly, as if you were serving the Lord, not people.
(Ephesians 6:7)

The mind governed by the flesh is death, but the mind governed by the Spirit is life and peace. (Romans 8:6)

Love the Lord your God with all your heart and with all your soul and with all your strength. (Deuteronomy 6:5)

And Samuel said to all the house of Israel, "If you are returning to the Lord with all your heart, then put away the foreign gods and the Ashtaroth from among you and direct your heart to the Lord and serve him only, and he will deliver you out of the hand of the Philistines."
(1 Samuel 7:3 esv)

The precepts of the LORD are right, giving joy to the heart. The commands of the LORD are radiant, giving light to the eyes. (Psalm 19:8)

"This is the covenant I will make with the people of Israel after that time," declares the LORD. "I will put my law in their minds and write it on their hearts. I will be their God, and they will be my people."

(Jeremiah 31:33)

REFLECTION QUESTIONS

Here are some reflection questions you might consider when evaluating and developing a life of teachability:

1. What does the story of Jonah teach us about following the leading of the Lord? Why was this so difficult for Jonah? What are some of God's teachings that are hard for you to follow?

2. When given reproach and warning, the people of Ninevah chose to obey God and turn from their wicked ways. Does Jonah's anger have any correlation to the Pharisees in the New Testament? Does it tell us anything about how some modern churches operate today?

3. What does the movie *Sister Act* show us about blooming where you are planted? Does this fictional story ring true? Are there examples in your life where you've seen God move through someone's faithful determination?

4. God's abundance is sometimes poured out later than we might desire. Bill Gaither's story illustrates a lifetime of faithful service before he finally realized his initial dream. Gaither would have chosen a life in quartet music years earlier, but it was only when he thought retirement was imminent that God brought to life the desires of Bill's heart. What does this story tell those of us who seem to be coming to the end of our usefulness or our journey? For a believer, is there any such thing as true retirement?

4

WAITING PRODUCTIVELY

(Luke 1)

When we've been going at full steam, trying to do everything right, setbacks and delays can leave us shaken. It feels like an eternity when we're told we must wait, it's not time yet, or we need to go through something first. Dealing with the unexpected consequences of those delays or failures can make us want to curl up inside ourselves until it's over or feels less brutal. It's normal to want to leave it all alone until the pain or disappointment passes or lessens. Sometimes that means we end up closing ourselves off from God, partially *checking out* for a while, or giving up on our goal and letting the doubts take over entirely. But none of those has to be our fate.

The waiting game can feel like failure. It's especially hard when our own mistakes led to the delay or setback. But waiting isn't the end. Waiting is an opportunity for something greater. If anything, it can sharpen us or increase our passion for whatever we are waiting on. Even when we're hurting, feel like we have less of a voice or less to give for a while, or are still reeling from an event or rejection, we can know that it is not the end of our story. We simply have to stay open to the opportunities we *do* have. They might be carrying us somewhere great; we just don't know it yet.

THE STORY OF ZECHARIAH

In the New Testament, there was a priest named Zechariah who was a righteous man in the sight of God. He and his wife, Elizabeth, devoutly obeyed all of the Lord's commands and were both very old but childless.

Priests were chosen by lot to burn incense in the temple of the Lord. It was quiet and contemplative time. Once, during Zechariah's turn, he was alone at the altar when an angel of the Lord suddenly appeared. Zechariah was in shock.

> But the angel said, "Don't be afraid, Zechariah! God has heard your prayer. Your wife, Elizabeth, will give you a son, and you are to name him John." (Luke 1:13 NLT)

Zechariah listened intently.

"John will bring you great joy and delight," the angel continued. "John will be great in the sight of the Lord."

What miraculous news! Zechariah stared in awe as the angel forged on with important instructions. "Never let John drink wine or fermented drink because he will have the Holy Spirit in him even before he is born. He will be an instrument of repentance for many. In fact, John will make the way ready for the coming of the Messiah."

Despite the angel's message and despite being known as a man of faith, Zechariah doubted his wife would be able to conceive.

Despite the personal messenger before him, despite the miracle of the angel's presence, and despite being known as a man of faith, Zechariah had his doubts. It seemed impossible, considering his age, his wife's age... The doubts overshadowed his faith, and he replied tentatively, "Are you sure, angel? My wife and I are very old."

This clearly was not the response the angel expected. The angel retorted:

I am Gabriel! I stand in the very presence of God. It was he who sent me to bring you this good news! (Luke 1:19 NLT)

The good news was about to become difficult news because Gabriel spoke again, doing something remarkable in response to Zechariah's doubts. "Since you didn't believe my words, which are true, you will now be silent and unable to speak until the child is born."

Life for Zechariah changed in an instant. What should have been a glorious day of celebration was now a reminder of his lack of faith, a lesson in trust, and the commencement of a long waiting game.

Meanwhile, the people outside the temple were waiting for Zechariah. When he finally emerged, they asked him why he had stayed so long inside, but when Zechariah opened his mouth, nothing came out. He couldn't tell them; he was unable to say anything at all. Gabriel's words echoed in Zechariah's mind. He gestured and made signs with his hands. Finally, the people realized that Zechariah had seen a vision in the temple.

Zechariah returned home at the end of his service week, and soon, his wife Elizabeth became pregnant. She was elated. "Look what God has done for me!" she said. "He's shown His favor!" Zechariah, of course, could say nothing.

When Elizabeth was six months into her pregnancy, the Lord sent the angel Gabriel to Nazareth to share good news with Elizabeth's cousin, Mary. The angel proclaimed that Mary would carry the Son of God. Pregnant with Jesus, the Virgin Mary went to see Elizabeth, and when she greeted her cousin, the baby leaped in Elizabeth's womb, and she was filled with the incredible Holy Spirit. Elizabeth cried to Mary, "Blessed are you, Mary, among women! Blessed is the child you bear! My baby leaped for joy at the sound of your voice! You have believed the Lord would fulfill His promises to you!"

"*And Mary said, 'My soul magnifies the Lord, and my spirit rejoices in God my Savior'*" (Luke 1:46 ESV). She began to praise God for all the good He had done. And still, Zechariah could say nothing. He couldn't offer his congratulations, couldn't celebrate aloud, couldn't offer words of kindness or wisdom.

A short time later, Elizabeth gave birth to a son. All of her relatives and neighbors rejoiced with her and Zechariah. It was a great celebration for everyone knew that the only way Elizabeth was able to have a child in her old age was through the grace of God.

When the time came to circumcise the child, there was much talk of naming the boy after Zechariah, but Elizabeth said, "No, he will be called John." The relatives disagreed, arguing, "No one in the family has been named John. Are you sure?" But Elizabeth held out. Zechariah got a writing tablet and surprised everyone by writing, "*His name is John*" (Luke 1:63).

As soon as he wrote these words, Zechariah's tongue was freed. He opened his mouth and began praising God. The neighbors were astonished. Soon everyone in the countryside was talking about all the wondrous things that had happened surrounding this birth. Everyone knew God had been at work. They knew there was something special about this newborn boy, John. They saw that the Lord's hand was upon him.

> *Everyone knew God had been at work and there was something special about this newborn boy, John.*

Once Zechariah had his voice back, he did not waste a moment in making up for lost time. He praised God and prophesied. He proclaimed that his son, "*because of the tender mercy of our God*" (Luke 1:78), would pave the way for the Christ. He said John would guide their feet onto the paths of peace.

The child grew, became strong in spirit, and lived in the wilderness until beginning his ministry in Israel. As John matured and began preparing the way for Jesus, he may have made some folks uneasy. John wore crazy clothes made from camel's hair. He only ate locusts and wild honey. He talked funny. But John's message was spot on. He preached of the coming salvation. He preached of One to follow.

All of this came from the righteous walk of Zechariah.

SETTING THE STAGE

The only way to step up is to speak up. But sometimes the only way God can get us to step up and speak up is to shut us up! To bring change to our lives in some way that gets our attention and reminds us of who He is. Zechariah's response was probably about the same as ours would be in a similar situation—doubting the message, thinking God wouldn't fully factor in all of the variables. (Newsflash: God knows your age. He knows the variables.)

So God's response to Zechariah was literally to shut him up. Initially this looks like some sort of punishment, but it is much more than that. God was creating a teachable moment for this priest. Zechariah's whole life was about words and communicating. As a priest, he was a leader in his community. He was respected, and people listened to him. He was even on the job in the temple when the angel appeared with the great news. Despite a life of service dedicated to the Lord and His people, Zechariah responded to God's messenger with skepticism. He got it wrong even though he had every reason to get it right.

The good news in all of this is that God knows us. He understands our hearts, desires, and motives intimately. God knew how Zechariah would respond, and it's likely that instead of being furious with him, God simply saw an opportunity, a teachable moment. It's like a parent who lets a child help out in the kitchen. The child may make mistakes and create a mess, but the time spent with the parent, learning and fellowshipping, is certainly worth the cost. Zechariah had made a mistake in not trusting God, and God saw a chance to work on his heart, a way to draw Zechariah closer to Him and reveal more of who He is.

By taking away Zechariah's voice, God got the priest's attention—and the attention of everyone who knew him. Like any priest or teacher, Zechariah would've been well-connected and in relationship with many people. Perhaps little boys turned and went the other way when they saw the preacher coming because they wanted to avoid another lesson. Others in town might have looked forward to receiving his insight and wisdom. Some may have been annoyed by Zechariah's constant preaching. Regardless, the people knew Zechariah as a communicator, and when his ability to speak was taken away, that would've been big news. Everyone would have known that something was up, something was going on.

> *What may have appeared to be a huge setback for Zechariah actually set the stage for John, who set the stage for Jesus.*

What may have appeared to Zechariah to be a huge setback, a debilitating consequence of failure, actually set the stage for John, who set the stage for Jesus. Because of Zechariah's forced silence and the miracle of John's birth, John was noticed and his future was already of interest. It was clear the hand of God was on his life. What may have seemed like a punishment was more like a huge drumroll announcing the coming of Christ.

Zechariah's self-identity could've been wrapped up in his position as well. We can't know this for sure, but perhaps God was doing more than just teaching Zechariah to trust in the miracle of his wife's late-in-life pregnancy and the birth of his son. Perhaps God was doing some heart work on him. That would mean a full nine months for God to move in Zechariah's heart and life in a new way—plenty of time for Zechariah to look inward and realize that it wasn't all about him.

A BLESSING IN DISGUISE

Our good friend Steve Casteel talks often of *marinating* in something—spending time to reflect and soak up all that needs to be taken in.

That's a good image for what the time of Elizabeth's pregnancy was for Zechariah. He was forced to be quiet and marinate in the presence of God.

Facing limitations and setbacks can sometimes help us grow in ways we never would have otherwise. They push us to reconsider what we've always done and the way our world has always been. They force us to see the world in a new light and approach it in ways we never would have considered. They force us to pause and slow down and behold what is in front of us.

How often could we use such a wake-up call? How often do we talk over God when He tries to speak to us? How hard is it for us to close our mouths from time to time so we can truly be still, be quiet in His presence, come to know Him, and see what He has in store for us? Like Zechariah, when our faith is really tested, we can find ourselves doubting when we should be trusting. We can find ourselves talking and questioning when we should be listening for His gentle whisper and entering into whatever He has in store for us with open ears and eyes.

How sweet it is to have a God who can close our mouths for our own sake. God did a work on Zechariah during his wife's pregnancy, and we can see it in Scripture. When Zechariah could finally talk again, there was a difference in his approach. The first thing he did was genuinely praise God and proclaim His goodness. Zechariah was not lifting up praises as a professional priest. He wasn't merely going through the motions and doing what was expected of him. No, this time, Zechariah gave the genuine praise of someone who has seen goodness fulfilled. The Bible says he was filled with the Holy Spirit and prophesied. This was the real deal, a joyful praise such as Zechariah had not known before. It was all the sweeter for having been silent in the presence of God.

Zechariah's failure taught him some things. Through his circumstances, he was forced to cultivate gifts that were already inside him. His failure forced him to un-fail. He marinated during that whole nine-month period while awaiting his son's birth and grew closer to God, emerging with a new perspective, a new walk. His wait was worth it.

Often, circumstances force us into periods of waiting. Unlike Zechariah, we may retain the ability to speak and communicate freely, but we might find it difficult to have meaningful things to say or not find life meaningful at all. We may find ourselves waiting for life to return to *normal* after a failure or setback. The danger during these times is choosing to be unproductive while waiting, but that's what this lesson attempts to teach us.

There is a difference between *sterile* waiting and *productive* waiting. Sterile waiting is when we put our lives on hold because we think God hasn't moved. Productive waiting is all about using the periods of stillness—the setbacks, letdowns, and unexpected anomalies that seem to shove us into a corner where it feels like there is no movement. It's about choosing to refocus on our calling, our mission, or maybe even what we could improve rather than focusing on the current challenges.

> *Productive waiting is all about choosing to refocus on our calling, our mission, or maybe even what we could improve.*

Periods of waiting are a gift. These times can be a break in the routine, a period to reflect and recalculate our trajectory, or a chance to get out of our comfort zone to learn something new. Setbacks can truly be a blessing in disguise. God gave such a gift to Zechariah, and though it took some work, Zechariah got the message. His walk with God became real during that time of waiting.

WAITING WITH PURPOSE

Abraham Lincoln is one of the most revered presidents in our nation's history—and a master of overcoming obstacles. As the sixteenth president, he basically single-handedly saved the union. Without his determination, drive, and leadership abilities, it is likely that America would look very different today. But because of his character traits, Lincoln is routinely listed by many as our greatest leader. However, Abraham Lincoln endured his share of failures or setbacks amid his accomplishments, including:

1. Lost job in 1832.

2. Defeated for state legislature in 1832.

3. Failed in business in 1833.

4. Elected to state legislature in 1834.

5. Sweetheart died in 1835.

6. Had nervous breakdown in 1836.

7. Defeated in run for state speaker in 1838.

8. Defeated in nomination for Congress in 1843.

9. Elected to Congress in 1846.

10. Lost renomination in 1848.

11. Rejected for land officer in 1849.

12. Defeated in run for US Senate in 1854.

13. Defeated in run for nomination as vice president in 1856.

14. Defeated in run for US Senate again in 1858.

15. Elected president of the United States in 1860.[15]

This list is pretty significant. Any combination of these struggles might have sent lesser men fast on their way to other pursuits. But Lincoln was different. He felt he had a destiny to serve and lead despite the many challenges he faced.

Lincoln had many lesser known accomplishments while he was waiting on the bigger things. He was elected company captain of his Illinois militia in the Black Hawk War. He was appointed as postmaster in New Salem and deputy surveyor of Sangamon County. He received almost no formal education but worked hard and was granted a law license. He practiced law in the US District Court.

Setbacks need not lead to defeat. The example of Lincoln's life is an encouraging one, which is why it is often used to illustrate overcoming failure. But some may overlook the fact that Lincoln was learning along the way; he was using the opportunity to un-fail with every failure he faced. He

---

15. "Lincoln's 'Failures'?", *Abraham Lincoln Online*, www.abrahamlincolnonline.org/lincoln/education/failures.htm. Compiled by Lucas Morel from the chronology in *Lincoln: Selected Speeches and Writings* by Abraham Lincoln, Don E. Fehrenbacher, ed. (New York: Vintage Books, 1992).

made use of his waiting time and learned endurance, patience, and tenacity. He learned compromise and focus. He learned enough to save a nation.

> *Abraham Lincoln kept learning while pursuing his destiny to serve and lead. He used every failure he faced as an opportunity to un-fail.*

Lincoln's flexibility and quick recovery allowed him to advance to the highest office in our country. With each obstacle, he simply doubled down with even greater focus. The drive to succeed and meet his calling was important to him. In fact, he ultimately gave his life to it.

Lincoln had premonitions and visions. He often dreamed of a fast-moving ship taking him to a dark, distant shore. In a way, Lincoln knew he was giving his life to a cause. But the cause was worth it to Lincoln. He had endured the defeats. He had spent the in-between times not in sterile waiting but in productive learning. When the time came, Lincoln saw the way through the bloody struggle that was the Civil War more clearly than most of those around him. Lincoln had been through many fires, and he knew how to endure and wait with purpose.

KEEP GOING

For a more recent example of waiting with intention, there's actor Ke Huy Quan, who waited over twenty years for an incredible comeback within the film industry. After seeing some success and attention as a teen for his roles in *Indiana Jones and the Temple of Doom* and *The Goonies*, he became disheartened when he didn't see many opportunities for Asian-Americans onscreen. For a while, he left acting behind for a film degree and alternative work behind the scenes. But when *Crazy Rich Asians* became a hit, Quan decided to try again, landed the role of Waymond Wang in *Everything Everywhere All at Once*, and walked away with the Academy Award for Best Supporting Actor, as well as a Golden Globe for Best Supporting Actor in a Motion Picture.

During his Oscar acceptance speech, he thanked his wife, saying, "I owe everything to the love of my life, my wife Echo, who month after month, year after year for twenty years told me that one day, one day my time will come." He waited for that moment. He yearned for that moment for so long. He added, "Dreams are something you have to believe in. I almost gave up on mine. To all of you out there, please keep your dreams alive."[16]

There will be delays, there will be obstacles, and there will be setbacks. However long they last, whether one week or twenty years, we can keep going and waiting for the moments God has in store for us.

Greta Gerwig—a well-known actress, playwright, screenwriter, producer, and director (think *Lady Bird*, *Little Women*, and *Barbie*)—initially faced overwhelming rejection, getting a "no thanks" from every graduate school she applied to. Unable to go in the direction she'd planned, this turn of events led her to make use of her skills with the opportunities available, which initially led her into the independent film world. She didn't let the schools' rejection stop her. She learned anyway and kept putting projects under her belt. She's now a household name and a sought-after director.

Gerwig has been nominated for major Academy Awards, BAFTA awards, Golden Globes, and more. She won a Golden Globe for Cinematic and Box Office Achievement for *Barbie*, for which she directed and co-wrote the screenplay.[17] Whether you're a fan of her movies or not, you can admire her grit and determination. She faced down her rejection, waited with intention, and has ended up hitting some major milestones in the movie industry.

Setbacks may be setting us up for something larger down the road if we keep moving forward and using that time.

---

16. Beth Harris, "Ke Huy Quan wins Oscar in an inspiring Hollywood comeback," *Associated Press*, March 13, 2023, apnews.com/article/oscars-2023-best-supporting-actor-dc a4e63731fc0bb41ded1e55c1210585.

17. Nicolas Vega, "Before 'Barbie', Oscar nominee Greta Gerwig was rejected by every writing program she applied to," CNBC *Make It*, March 10, 2024, www.cnbc.com/2024/03/06/oscars-2024-greta-gerwig-was-rejected-by-every-grad-school-she-applied-to.html.

HOLD FAST

Silence can be as overwhelming as noise. And waiting on God when He's silent can feel intolerable. Waiting for our dreams to come true, for something to come together, for a next step to finally be taken … all of it can seem painfully drawn out. Even the most resilient dreamer may want to give up.

Sometimes we must completely surrender the things we know about ourselves and about life, but we also must surrender those things we don't even understand—the failures, the setbacks, the weaknesses, the doubts, the anticipation, the fears, the waiting, the timeline expectation we didn't even know we had. We must give everything to God, saying, "God, even if You give me the most amazing future, I will give it back to You in return."

Waiting can feel like the end of the world,
but sometimes it is just the beginning.

It may feel like punishment, but it can be a blessing to take a step back and interact with the world in a different way. Waiting can feel like the end of the world, but sometimes it is just the beginning. In the meantime, we need to keep believing, keep our focus, find the beauty in our period of waiting, and grow the strength and skills we'll need for the future. That is how we un-fail. That is how we become ready to do the tasks that God has set before us.

SCRIPTURE TOOLS

The word is very near you. It is in your mouth and in your heart, so that you can do it. (Deuteronomy 30:14 ESV)

Joyful are those who listen to me, watching for me daily at my gates, waiting for me outside my home! (Proverbs 8:34 NLT)

Be like men who are waiting for their master to come home from the wedding feast, so that they may open the door to him at once when he comes and knocks.   (Luke 12:36 ESV)

Blessed are those servants whom the master finds awake when he comes. Truly, I say to you, he will dress himself for service and have them recline at table, and he will come and serve them.

(Luke 12:37 ESV)

Now the prize awaits me—the crown of righteousness, which the Lord, the righteous Judge, will give me on the day of his return. And the prize is not just for me but for all who eagerly look forward to his appearing.   (2 Timothy 4:8 NLT)

In keeping with his promise we are looking forward to a new heaven and a new earth, where righteousness dwells.   (2 Peter 3:13)

You are looking forward to the coming of God's Son from heaven—Jesus, whom God raised from the dead. He is the one who has rescued us from the terrors of the coming judgment.

(1 Thessalonians 1:10 NLT)

REFLECTION QUESTIONS

Here are some reflection questions you might consider when evaluating and developing a life of productive waiting:

1. Why did a priest who taught the power of God have such trouble believing that God was sending him a child?

2. Zechariah was struck silent during Elizabeth's pregnancy. What effect would this period of waiting have upon Elizabeth and the community?

3. When he could speak again, Zechariah's first words were praise to God. How would the praise lifted up by a new parent be different, perhaps, than that of a seasoned priest? What times in your life has God been more real to you than in other times?

4. Abraham Lincoln, Ke Huy Quan, and Greta Gerwig all kept moving forward when they faced rejection, finding new opportunities to use their talents and skills. What times in your life have you faced a limitation or setback, forcing you to go in a different direction? In what ways did you grow in those times? How did God help you through them?

SECTION TWO: AVOIDING PITFALLS

We know that no matter where we begin, we will all face failure and setbacks. We've seen the foundations to maneuver onto the road of forgiveness and restoration, start accepting our failures, and learn how to wait on God. Now, let's talk about the potential pitfalls.

Yes, problems will arise and failures will happen, but what if we could prevent some of them? What if we looked at how our daily decisions and reactions to the world around us affected our lives on a grander scale?

NBC launched *Late Night with David Letterman* in 1982. The program was a quirky mix of candid interviews, hip music, crazy stunts, and the occasional throwing of things off tall buildings to see (in wonderful slow motion) how they would splaaat when hitting the ground. *Late Night* followed the more conservative *Tonight Show* with Johnny Carson, and it became a great hit. While older adults went to sleep watching Carson, the highly sought-after college student demographic stayed up to watch the antics of Letterman, his band, and his cronies.

The program was owned by Johnny Carson's production company. This was a great thing for Letterman since Carson was his hero. There was no bigger influence on the young host than the legendary Johnny Carson. Letterman had appeared on the *Tonight Show* numerous times and eventually served as a semi-permanent guest host. He had a great relationship with his idol, and Letterman dreamed of one day being promoted from *Late Night* to become the full-time host of America's all-time top nighttime talk program.

There was a problem though. Letterman had always been a bit of a rebel. Sure, he had great respect and admiration for Carson, but that respect did not transfer to the executives of NBC. The contempt Letterman had for the "network pinheads" was a source of contention throughout the ten-year run of Letterman's show on NBC. He routinely made fun of network executives on the air, even to the point of showing their photos and berating them. These jabs went over extremely well with the college student viewers across the nation; they did not, however, please the powerful men at the network.

All of this bad blood affected the outcome of who was selected to replace Carson when he retired in 1992. Letterman felt he'd done his own program for ten long years in preparation for the move up to the *Tonight Show*. He felt it was a strong resume; *Late Night* had made significant sums of money for NBC. Plus, it was Letterman's dream to replace Carson. It came as a tremendous blow to him when the network chose to give the position to Jay Leno instead. Letterman was so devastated that he left the network. He produced a new program for CBS called the *Late Show*. Letterman stayed at CBS until his own retirement in 2015.

Being on television for thirty-three years is no small consolation prize. Letterman was the hero of many late-night followers after his run, just as Carson had been the role model for Letterman. But none of these things compensated Letterman for not getting the *Tonight Show*. Letterman being passed over was directly due to the host's many years of taunting behavior, despite his contribution to the network.

What we're choosing to do today matters. How we approach our relationships, our jobs, our day-to-day, our dreams, our lives overall—it all matters.

The little things can make or break us over time. They can help set us up for success or slowly grind us down. If we can prevent some of our failures and their effects by staying mindful of our actions, by keeping an eye on the everyday, by staying solid during the mundane, we will already be on the road to un-failing.

We need to vision-cast, to look forward. Frankly, we need to dream. It can drive our work ethic and make us tenacious toward achieving a goal. However, it is important to remember that our daily walk, the journey we travel while looking ahead, is important. The small decisions we make today can help or harm us tomorrow.

5

REFINING THE EAR

(Genesis 3)

We all crave community, acceptance, and fitting in, whether we like it or not. Community and connection in and of itself is an incredible aspect of human life. That we were created to commune with other people on intense levels with extreme emotions is really an incredible gift that can be an endless source of inspiration, validation, and comfort. We were made to live dynamic and passionate lives.

But there's another side to all of it.

Many of us like to think of ourselves as resilient to the input and suggestions of other people, especially when those suggestions could hurt us or someone else. In reality, however, we take in a lot more than we realize. We are not as hardy and unwavering as we sometimes like to think we are. There is a darker aspect to our craving for community and being part of the group.

We can let too much soak in. We may fail to filter out the unnecessary—or worse yet, the harmful. This has been true since the beginning of human life on earth, and it's true for us today. In order to live joyful lives of integrity, we have to learn how to maneuver through the world's incessant input and filter out what doesn't serve us. The consequences of not doing so can be harsh and lasting, as humanity learned very early on.

THE STORY OF ADAM AND EVE

Let's start at the very beginning...

From the dust of the earth, God formed man and breathed life into Adam, and he became a living being. This was the pinnacle of the creation process. God had spent a busy week creating the heavens and the earth, the night and the day, the animals, and everything we see in this stunning world of nature. The wonders and majesty were boundless and astounding. God saw that it was good. And yet He wasn't finished.

Creating man with a living soul, with free will, with all of his intricate wonder, was something God saved for last. And in that creation, He saw that it was very good. Then He added some final touches. He was a grand artist, putting just the right strokes on the canvas to form highlights. He painted a garden called Eden just for Adam. There were trees pleasing to the eye and abundant with food. It was paradise. And yet something was missing.

He created the heavens and earth and saw that they were good. He shaped the animals and trees and knew that they were good. He formed man and knew that he was good. The garden was good. It was all good.

But then God saw that something else was needed. God knew, *"It is not good for the man to be alone"* (Genesis 2:18).

From the very first chapters of Scripture, we see the sacred mystery of the Trinity doing Their thing, working miracles in an interconnected relationship.

This is significant. From the very first chapters of Scripture—literally the first verses of Genesis 1—we see the sacred mystery of the Trinity doing Their thing, working miracles in an interconnected relationship. That is the image in which we were created, the sweet, subtle nature of God's own personality being made known. We are meant to have relationship and community. It is woven into the spiritual, relational, and emotional DNA of our existence. And so, looking down at Adam, God knew that there was an incompleteness to him.

So, what did God do? He decided to make a suitable companion for Adam. With one of Adam's ribs, God formed woman and brought her to life, flesh of Adam's flesh, bone of Adam's bone. (See Genesis 2:23.)

From the beginning, we can see that God's intention is for us to do life together—literally. We are a part of each other. We are one. We are formed in the image of our Creator.

Community is vital. It is through community that we are able to feel complete and whole. The presence of others soothes and uplifts us. The words of others inspire, fortify, and heal. Without this, we are unable to have the whole picture or see the complete work of God. But being in community, being part of society and interacting with other people, automatically puts us in a vulnerable position.

Because listening to others can be tricky.

Along with all the good voices that make creation so whole and perfect, there are (and were) other voices—ones without our best interests in mind that wander freely through our lives.

From the first, God told Adam not to eat of the fruit from the tree in the middle of the garden. This command was not given lightly. In fact, God warned, "If you eat from it, you will die." (See Genesis 2:17.) Adam had no problem with this. God said it, and Adam listened. Then along came Eve. She, too, found it easy to obey what God had commanded. She left the fruit of the forbidden tree alone, and for a time, all was well in paradise. Adam and Eve walked and talked with God and enjoyed sweet communion together.

All was well until another voice entered the picture.

> *Now the serpent was more crafty than any of the wild animals the*
> *LORD God had made. He said to the woman, "Did God really say,*
> *'You must not eat from any tree in the garden'?"*   (Genesis 3:1)

His was not the voice of a friend. It was manipulation from the start, a sowing of unrest and dissatisfaction. The serpent continued with a lie. "You will certainly not die," he said to the woman. "God knows that if you eat from that tree, your eyes will be opened and you'll be as smart as God; you'll know good and evil."

Eve looked at the tree. It was beautiful. She thought about the serpent's words. Of course she desired wisdom—was that such a bad thing? Surely it would be okay. Surely she was missing out on something she deserved, something she ought to have. So she took the fruit and ate. Then, wanting Adam to experience the same awakening, she shared it with him.

The serpent had convinced the couple to eat the forbidden fruit. He had coaxed them into disobeying God's one directive in the garden, and all it had taken was a simple twisting of the truth. For surely they did have an awakening, but it wasn't the one they'd expected.

Ever since Adam and Eve, we've been battling the lie that we
can choose what is best for ourselves rather than
heeding the words of God.

It was the first lie—the lie that tells us we are sufficient to make these decisions, to choose what is best for ourselves rather than heeding the words of God. And it is this very lie that we have been battling ever since. Adam and Eve felt this change right away. Trading obedience for the lie changed their relationship with the Father. Nothing would ever be the same.

This time, when they heard God walking toward them among the trees, for the first time, they hid themselves from Him. They avoided His presence.

One small moment in time, one conversation that sunk in, got under Eve's skin and redirected her course of action, and then everything changed.

Today we find ourselves bombarded more than ever with enticing messages and haughty permission to do wrong. The information age invites us to know more, to be as smart as God—the same offer the serpent made in Genesis 3. Crafty voices radiate from television and media, telling us to chase after happiness and do what feels right *to us*, whatever that means. We scroll through our screens and bring more and more and more words before us, words that shape and form who and what we are.

If we're not careful, we can find ourselves slipping into the same lie: the lie that we know better than God.

HARDWIRED TO LISTEN

A pediatrician friend once noted, "Babies are born with their ears wide open." After nine months in the snug, warm womb, it is a shock to enter the world with all of its sudden lights, noise, and chaos. It may take a few days for newborns to get the feel of what they are seeing and experiencing, but one sense that is in full working mode from the start is their hearing. None of us can remember back that far, so we can only imagine what it feels like to be new to the world again, but there have to be so many unfamiliar sounds bombarding a newborn. Even the familiar sound of mother's voice would be louder, more jarring.

As we mature into children and then young adults, our dynamic of listening is much the same. We start off taking in everything at face value, and over time, we start to filter through the onslaught. Some of the voices and opinions soften while others become stronger.

Through the journey of growing and developing, many of our positive and negative interactions are the result of who we listen to for guidance and wisdom. And as the old principle states, "What goes in must come out." If we listen to garbage—to hatred, bigotry, selfishness, and other negative thoughts and emotions—that garbage will find its way back into our own words, attitudes, and perceptions. If we listen to words that uplift and encourage, they pay dividends of hope and strength. What goes in will eventually come out, in some way or another.

Humans have a need for deep, interpersonal connections. Journalist Geoff Colvin states, "We are social beings, hardwired from our evolutionary past to equate personal relationships with survival."[18] Of course, as people of faith, we believe this need is more than an evolutionary accident, but rather part of the delicate imprint of the Creator on the human experience. However, when this need becomes endangered by disruptive circumstances or relationships—when we surround ourselves with and listen to the wrong people—our entire lives can become upended. Just as God created us to be in community, He also offers us discernment. Be careful that you're not listening to the wrong people.

> *When we surround ourselves with and listen to the wrong people, our entire lives can become upended.*

Despite their track record of walking with God, Adam and Eve were willing to give up everything they knew once they were offered an opportunity to glorify themselves. Think about that! How many times had God come walking in the cool of the day to be in fellowship with Adam and Eve? They had no reason or evidence that God would disappoint them, yet the serpent convinced them that there was a better way. They let the serpent's voice overpower the voice of God. All it took was a new voice sneaking in and slipping them a new, tempting idea, saying it was all okay.

We can't entirely stop these voices from arriving in our lives in the first place, but we can choose whether or not we listen to them, whether we give them more opportunities and consideration. We can choose whether we let them guide our lives or not.

WORDS OF HEALING

Dr. James Merlino of the famed Cleveland Clinic developed a revolutionary program that trains every team member of the clinic, from the physicians to the support staff, in empathy and relationship building. The

---

18. Geoff Colvin, "Humans Are Underrated," *Fortune*, August 1, 2015, 112.

clinic discovered that since human interaction is key to an organization and its mission, it only takes one wrongly placed human to disrupt the system.

Colvin writes:

> The evidence is clear that the most effective groups are those whose members most strongly possess the most essentially, deeply human abilities—empathy above all, social sensitivity, storytelling, collaborating, solving problems together, building relationships.[19]

Appropriate listening skills are critical.

Our friend Jack lived one of the most accomplished, successful lives one could imagine. He had been a star student and athlete in the small Alabama town where he grew up. His father, the local town doctor, molded Jack into a young man of character, faith, and ambition. Little in Jack's life seemed out of reach.

Jack graduated with honors from the University of Alabama and finished at the top of his law school class at Vanderbilt. Along the way, he met and married Betty, the love of his life. After law school, they moved to New York, where Jack interned at a local law firm, before finally settling in Betty's hometown of Memphis, Tennessee. Jack's legal career was fast-paced, the stuff of most young attorneys' dreams. By the time Jack was forty, he had traded law for banking and finance, becoming president of one of the largest banks in Tennessee. Several mergers later, the now multi-billion-dollar financial institution, one of the largest in the United States, named Jack chairman and CEO.

By 2006, Jack was the father of three grown children and the grandfather of a growing brood. He played tennis and golf, not just on the weekends or at business outings, but at a competitive amateur level. He was considered one of the best in both sports for his age group in the Mid-South. With a growing family and a growing business career, the narrative of Jack's life seemed written in the stars.

This was all about to change.

---

19. Ibid., 106.

Jack noticed a physical numbness and found himself struggling for words for several days but thought little of it. His fast-paced life—with homes in Birmingham, Alabama; Memphis; and Sea Island, Georgia, not to mention the constant travel involved in managing one of the country's largest investment banks—would have drained much younger men. But Jack's symptoms were more than fatigue. They were the onset of a massive stroke.

Within days of the first signs, Jack had lost use of his left side and experienced a significant speech impediment. His impaired mobility rendered this constantly moving man a prisoner in his own body. Jack remembers his first conversations with loved ones, pastors, and colleagues.

"Everyone was so supportive, but you could tell by the looks on their faces that it was very serious," Jack says. "You keep hoping that what you are experiencing feels or seems bad because of how you are perceiving it, but when you see your wife or daughter's eyes fill with tears while you try to form the simplest of words, you know this is bigger than anything you have faced before."

But Jack had an incredibly supportive collection of family and friends. And of course, as a man of great faith, his own tenacious spirit provided a unique strength for whatever came next. However, *next* for people in his condition was limited. Phase one was making sure there weren't any more strokes, and phase two constituted relearning even the simplest of tasks, from buttoning a shirt and enunciating words to standing. These were the constant battles of Jack's first days and weeks following the stroke. Returning to work and resuming his former life was not part of the conversation. And he learned something valuable in the midst of it.

"When you are in those moments, being so vulnerable and at the mercy of so many others for the basic tasks of life," Jack says, "who you are listening to—I mean really listening to—may be the difference between learning to get by and prevailing against this monumental load of sorrow and suffering that has landed on you and your family." The tipping point of actually succeeding and making it through could come down to whose words he was truly taking to heart.

Jack remembers the day when he realized that the difference in how he felt, both emotionally and physically, was based on the scope of conversations he had with people around him. "If the conversation was about pity or frustration, I felt it, not just mentally, but almost in my bones," Jack relates. "But when people talked about healing ... taking the next hill ... it shaped more than just my rehab or medical status. It framed every part of me." Words could burn or they could carry him through.

Jack's eventual rehabilitation and return to work were not easy or simple. He faced his share of setbacks and obstacles, some of which his doctors, friends, and family thought were almost insurmountable. But by the time Jack retired some five years later, he had not only returned to work but had navigated the investment bank through the financial crisis of 2007, emerging as one of the stronger financial institutions in the country.

Today, Jack's mobility challenges him every day. He has dealt with a myriad of peripheral issues experienced by most stroke patients. The road has not been straight but filled with potholes, U-turns, sharp curves, bumps, sudden stops, and various other setbacks and challenges. And yet, Jack retired as one of the country's most successful and respected leaders. He then left high finance for the world of philanthropy and service, guiding various institutions and programs he loves, from Vanderbilt Law School to the Crimson Tide of Alabama (serving as chair of the President's Council) to executive council chairman of his local church. Jack also returned to playing golf on a regular basis, albeit at a much different level than before. Now, he mostly stretches his legs either chasing his grandchildren or running from their adorable, loving schemes and mischief.

When something out of his control failed him, positive conversations were a determining factor in putting Jack's life back on the road to success. Listening to the right people helped not just his mind but his *entire body* in the process of un-failing. Jack's story is evidence that life unfolds best against the backdrop of listening to faithful, sage advice and deciding to live it out with every part of our being.

DISCERNMENT THAT LOOKS BEYOND

Being a good listener is not only essential for our own well-being, but it also helps to make us effective leaders, friends, spouses, or employees. Listening well means understanding and effectively using discernment, the ability to sift through the chorus of voices and pay attention to the right ones. Plenty of conversations are competing for our attention. Some may be critical, but some will just be noise. Others will be intent on leading us in their own preferred direction. It takes practice, experience, and wisdom to truly understand that it isn't always the loudest voices that should gain our attention. We must be listening all the time so that we can discern the good from the bad.

> *It takes practice, experience, and wisdom to understand that it isn't always the loudest voices that should gain our attention.*

Rarely has there been a time in history when the delineation of good versus evil could be seen more clearly than in fighting the Nazis in World War II. Looking back now at the shocking footage filmed in the concentration camps easily convinces any good Christian that this evil regime absolutely had to be stopped. However, this wasn't as clear for the president of the United States in the late 1930s.

Franklin Delano Roosevelt did not know all of the extreme horrors that the Jewish people faced at the time America entered the war. Yes, persecution was taking place, but the real extent of the damage was yet unknown. We didn't have any news films or photos then to show us what was really happening. Roosevelt did know, however, that German Chancellor Adolf Hitler's aggression had to be stopped. FDR knew that without help, all of Europe would soon fall. And he knew that if England fell, the world would change drastically.

Still, Roosevelt had many voices in his ear. Some leaders called for isolationism, claiming that we should never again get into the affairs of Europe and lose the lives of our own young men as we did in World War I. Others said we couldn't afford to help—the Great Depression was still a vivid, recent reminder that we, too, were vulnerable. Many said interfering in Europe would be the doom of our own country. The voices hammering at Roosevelt were loud and persuasive.

But he heard the voice of another leader as well. British Prime Minister Winston Churchill flatly stated that without American assistance, Europe would fall and never recover. Churchill managed to persuade Roosevelt that isolation would profit us in the short term, but losing the war to Hitler would threaten the United States forever after. It was a compelling argument.

Though Roosevelt found that he agreed with Churchill, he knew he couldn't plunge the United States into immediate war. As a leader, Roosevelt kept his ears open to the many different arguments of his people and knew any decision would have ramifications. He also knew that something had to be done to provide assistance, so Roosevelt developed the Lend-Lease Act. America sent supplies, arms, planes, tanks, and other support to help Great Britian in their fight. This was not the United States entering the war, but it was *something*.

As time went on, Churchill constantly pushed for more help, while the American isolationists continued to shout for us to mind our own business. The clamoring was real and the pressure from both sides was enormous. Roosevelt, though, listened to his own inner voice that said we must keep helping in some way. He knew deep down that it was the right thing to do.

Eventually, Japan attacked Pearl Harbor, and we were plunged directly into the war. With our assistance, the conflict was won. The world owes a huge debt to Franklin Roosevelt, who kept his ears open to the many viable arguments but listened to the right voices in the end. Courage and discernment look beyond the immediate wins; they look at what is required for the long haul.

PRACTICE MAKES PERFECT

Adam and Eve got it wrong in a big way—and we aren't much different. By listening to what *we* want instead of trusting God, we continue the same patterns. But the good news is that their mistake, their failure, was not the end. Our mistakes don't have to be either. Humanity's first big failure provides us with a crucial lesson on listening that can reshape each one of us to live more in step with God so that we don't stumble as often. And even when we do, listening to the right people can help us on the road to un-failing and getting back in step quickly.

Following Jesus means listening to and learning from the very best and wisest sources—and then sharing that wisdom in an effective, valuable way. A friend who read an early version of this manuscript put it this way: "Listen to the right people, and then become one of those 'right people' to whom others should listen."

Listening to the right people can help us on the road to un-failing and getting back in step quickly.

The first step is simply to listen. Listen for God's voice amidst all of the noise. Read His Word. Discernment won't come overnight. It takes practice. You won't always get it right, but over time, you will find your ear refined to be a wise discerner of the voice of God, and the path forward will become a little bit clearer.

SCRIPTURE TOOLS

My dear brothers and sisters, take note of this: Everyone should be quick to listen, slow to speak and slow to become angry. (James 1:19)

Listen to advice and accept instruction, that you may gain wisdom in the future. (Proverbs 19:20 ESV)

To answer before listening—that is folly and shame. (Proverbs 18:13)

And we also thank God continually because, when you received the word of God, which you heard from us, you accepted it not as a human word, but as it actually is, the word of God, which is indeed at work in you who believe. (1 Thessalonians 2:13)

He answered them, "My mother and my brothers are those who hear the word of God and do it." (Luke 8:21 ESV)

Then a cloud appeared and covered them, and a voice came from the cloud: "This is my Son, whom I love. Listen to him!" (Mark 9:7)

"I tell you the truth, anyone who sneaks over the wall of a sheepfold, rather than going through the gate, must surely be a thief and a robber! But the one who enters through the gate is the shepherd of the sheep. The gatekeeper opens the gate for him, and the sheep recognize his voice and come to him. He calls his own sheep by name and leads them out. After he has gathered his own flock, he walks ahead of them, and they follow him because they know his voice. They won't follow a stranger; they will run from him because they don't know his voice." (John 10:1–5 NLT)

REFLECTION QUESTIONS

Here are some reflection questions you might consider when evaluating and developing a life of faithful listening:

1. Who do you tend to listen to for knowledge, expertise, and wise advice? Make a list and describe the nature of each relationship. Give examples of what you have learned from them. This can be a very eye-opening experience.

2. Why does God call the creation of man and woman "very good"? What is the difference between God's "good" and His "very good"? What does that say about how God values relationship?

3. Spend a few moments listing the most important relationships in your life. Are they healthy? How do you communicate most effectively in those relationships? What is the most unhealthy form of communication?

4. What is the first question God asks of Adam and Eve? Why does this have such an emotional feel to it?

5. Think of the reactions of Adam and Eve once God confronts them. Why do these reactions seem so familiar and personal? Describe, draw a picture, write a poem or a song—something with deep emotion—about God's reaction and response to humanity's first failure.

6

WATCHING OUR TONGUES

(Genesis 9)

Words have power. We see this over and over in Scripture. We saw it first in the tragic story of the garden when Adam and Eve listened to the serpent rather than God, but the theme continues. Because it's not just about discerning other people's words; it's also about the words *we* use and offer to other people. What comes out of our mouths can shape our lives and the lives of others for better or for worse, and the effects of those words can linger for generations.

Words, both good and bad, matter.

THE STORY OF NOAH

We see Adam and Eve expelled from paradise with their days numbered after listening to the serpent, and just a few pages further in the Old Testament, we find the story of Noah. In Noah's day, the Lord saw the wickedness and depravity of the human race, and Scripture says God's heart was troubled. It was so bad, He regretted even having placed man on the earth. But then it says something pretty great: there was a man named Noah, and *"Noah found favor in the eyes of the LORD"* (Genesis 6:8).

God had an affinity for this man who walked faithfully. Having made the decision to destroy the world, God tasked Noah with the building of a great ark to save himself, his family, and a whole lot of animals. God said, *"I will establish my covenant with you"* (Genesis 6:18). So Noah built the ark and did everything as God commanded him.

After God sealed Noah's family and all the animals in the finished ark, the earth was destroyed by forty days and forty nights of rain. In modern times, we see news footage of rising rivers, oceans, and hurricanes. Without having to experience it, we get to see the amazing force and power of surging water. Imagine a scene in which the rain pours down in sheets and the water does not stop rising. It just keeps coming and overtaking everything. Imagine the water covering the trees, the hills, the mountains, until nothing is left but the pouring, surging water. Imagine Noah and his family crammed in with the animals, waiting for the water to recede as the ark rocks about on the unfathomable, worldwide sea.

Finally, the flooding stopped, and the ark came to rest on top of a mountain. After waiting for the land to dry, which some say took over a year, the family disembarked with new instructions for a new world. Noah's three sons and their wives were to repopulate the earth.

Worshipping God, Noah built an altar and filled it with burnt offerings. God was pleased and pronounced a precious covenant with this man who had repeatedly done as He commanded. For Noah's sake, for his faithfulness throughout the storm, God promised to never again curse the ground because of man. Although man is evil, no matter how bad he becomes, God promised to never again cause flooding to destroy all living things.

Then, the Master Artist added some beautiful strokes of the brush: God painted a rainbow to seal the deal. Noah saw it. His sons—Shem, Ham, and Japheth—saw it too. We still see it today and are reminded of God's covenant, God's words. In this part of the story, words are a beautiful promise. They lock in the future of mankind with hope and assurance for the coming generations.

This is the setting in which we see our next lesson in failure.

Noah and his sons had dominion over the earth. He'd saved the animals, he'd found favor with the Lord, and now Noah was working in his vineyard. He drank some of the wine, the fruit of his labors ... and found himself drunk. He passed out, naked in his tent.

Ham, Noah's youngest son and the father of Canaan, walked in on Noah and discovered him in this embarrassing position. Rather than help his father cover up and maintain some dignity, Ham chose to step back out of the tent, where he immediately went and told his brothers Shem and Japheth.

Ham could have easily covered his naked father and helped hide Noah's shame, but he chose to tell his brothers about it instead.

It's not clear in the Bible why Ham did this or what he hoped to get out of it. He could have easily covered his father and helped hide Noah's shame. He could have kept it all a secret. But he chose not to.

The other brothers didn't hesitate. They took a garment, put it across their shoulders, and walked backward into the tent to avoid looking at their father in his disgraceful state. Once they'd eased their way in, they covered Noah's nakedness with the robe.

When Noah awoke from his stupor, he discovered what his youngest son had done. Noah was embarrassed. He was frustrated. And he did exactly what some of us might do in that same situation: he lashed out.

"Curse you, Ham, and you Canaan!" Noah yelled. "You'll be the lowest of slaves to your brothers!"

Not only did Noah curse Ham, but then he immediately turned around, blessed Shem, and asked for God's expansion of Japheth's territories.

In his shame and embarrassment, in the heat of the moment, Noah changed the lives of his children (and his children's children) forever— some for the better, but others distinctly for the worse. All because of an embarrassing situation he'd allowed himself to get into in the first place. The future of generations turned onto a new course in one hungover, thoughtless, emotional instant.

The Bible says Noah lived three hundred and fifty years after the flood, a grand total of nine hundred and fifty years before dying. And in all those many years, Noah never saw fit to forgive his youngest son. You might say at that moment, Noah was a cranky old man, or that his son was brazen and reckless. But Noah's words still mattered. They would still take hold and shape the future of Ham's descendants, creating deep-seated distrust and anger. In his weakness, Noah's words, both blessings and curses, had enduring consequences.

A LASTING EFFECT

Our words not only have immense power in the present moment but also generational effects. Stories and rumors are passed down. People take on labels, entire cultures are stereotyped, and before you know it, an off-hand comment becomes a way of regularly perceiving others and turns into the norm.

> *Before you know it, an offhand comment becomes a way of regularly perceiving others and turns into the norm.*

Noah's account illuminates the power of words on each end of the spectrum: both the value of good words and the potential harm in phrases thrown out in anger or carelessness. Noah's words carried over all the way to the promised land and beyond, when the Israelites saw the Canaanites (Ham's generational line) as inferior. Noah's temporary loss of control—his angry curse—had shocking power even after thirty generations. Ham's descendants became a line of servants. And all of this because Ham stayed a little too long in the tent, took a joke a little too far, and enjoyed shaming his father a little too much. Thus Noah lashed out.

What happened between Noah and Ham didn't stop there. After the curse, the descendants of Noah dispersed, going in different directions. Noah's anger broke the relationships this family had previously held close. Soon after, God separated them even further by causing them to speak multiple languages at the Tower of Babel. In a very real way, we can say that from that one incident—the shame of Noah—people all over the world now have a hard time understanding each other, creating significant divisions.

How many families don't speak a common language? How many families are not able to communicate love, affection, or generosity? How many of us are still broken by the words we speak or don't speak? How many of us are unable to get over the wrongs of the past and reconcile?

That was the case with Noah's family, and it is often the case for us. Noah's weakness resulted in generational pain and mistrust within his family. Within our own families, we often allow our weaknesses or bad behavior to have a lasting effect on those we love.

Just ask Paula Deen about the importance of choosing our words carefully. The Southern chef was a longtime favorite on the Food Network. It's little wonder—the episodes of her hit television program, *Paula's Home Cooking*, were full of great Southern cuisine with a huge dose of wit and humor thrown in for seasoning. Deen built a simple cooking program into a culinary empire that encompassed books, multiple television programs, restaurants, merchandise, and more. Sure, she started many recipes with a whole stick of butter, but fans and viewers ate it up ... until the sponsors left and the Food Network pulled Paula Deen off the channel.

Why did they do it? Deen's choice of words.

The interesting thing about this scenario is that Paula Deen had allegedly spoken the offensive words over twenty years earlier. Back then, she had used racial slurs while referring to an employee. Brought up two decades later, it was enough to bring down an entire kingdom.

The sins of the past tripped up the television star. Our words—whether spoken angrily, in error, or flippantly—can come back to haunt us.

Should Noah have forgiven Ham if his son had repented? We think so. Should Paula Deen be forgiven if she is sincerely remorseful and has learned from her mistakes and changed? Absolutely. Does that mean she will ever face the same opportunity to have such a large platform from which to communicate to others? Probably not.

Like the story of Noah, with Paula Deen, there were generational effects. Through Paula Deen's program, her sons had become personalities on the Food Network with a show of their own. The collapse of the sponsors for their mother also seemed to spell the end of the program for the Deen brothers. Her words affected their lives too.

A similar generational effect can be seen in the troubles of Bernie Madoff, father of the Ponzi scheme that cost investors fifty billion dollars. Although his sons exposed the scheme, the sins of their father came crashing down upon the family. One son died of cancer while the other died by suicide. For a time after his arrest, Bernie Madoff's wife changed her name, dyed her hair, and went into hiding. Although not directly responsible for either son's demise, Madoff's actions changed the life courses of his entire family.

Ham's actions affected his children and his children's children. Noah's words had ramifications for his entire family for generations to come. Our words and deeds are important, not only for us, but for all those we know and love. We must be careful with them.

> *Our words and deeds are important, not only for us, but for all those we know and love.*

The authors of this book were born and raised in the beautiful state of Mississippi. Before the American Civil War, Mississippi had more millionaires per capita than any other state. This, of course, was due to the fact that plantation owners did not have to pay wages to their black slaves; they got to keep all of the income for themselves. Ever since that war ended, Mississippi has been the poorest state in the nation. There are numerous reasons for this, but perhaps the biggest factor is that there was punishment for the evil of slavery. Mississippi continues to pay for the sins of the past. Our words and actions have ramifications, sometimes for generations to come.

THE INEVITABLE

One of Mississippi's favorite sons is author William Faulkner. There is pride in the fact that one of the most educationally challenged states in America produced such a prolific and acclaimed writer. He won the 1949 Nobel Prize for Literature, two Pulitzer Prizes for Fiction, and many other honors and awards. Faulkner is regarded as one of the nation's literary greats. And yet there is so much that was broken in this man's life.

One such area of pain can be found in Faulkner's relationship with his daughter, Jill.

It could not have been easy being Faulkner's child. On good days, the author could be the life of the party. But then there were the other days. There were periods when work on a novel went slowly, and he had to write scripts in Hollywood just to make money. In these times, Faulkner became another person. He was reclusive, private, and could be harsh to those around him. He could make cutting remarks that left a path of destruction in his wake.

Many times, the fuel for these outbursts came from a bottle. Faulkner's love for drinking is legendary. He was once asked how he could go so long drinking without eating anything. His response was, "There's a lot of nourishment in an acre of corn." But with such extreme consumption of alcohol, there was often no telling what Faulkner might say to those around him.

In an award-winning documentary produced by Mississippi Public Broadcasting in the 1970s, Jill Faulkner Summers was interviewed about her father. What came through in the film was evidence of a strained relationship between the two. She even spoke of his alcoholism. Once, she said, when Faulkner was already pretty tipsy from drinking, the young Jill asked her Pappy to stop drinking. Without missing a beat, Faulkner turned to her and said coldly, "You know, no one remembers Shakespeare's child."[20]

---

20. *William Faulkner: A Life on Paper*, directed by Robert Squier (1979; Mississippi Public Broadcasting).

Ouch. There is no way this unkind remark would ever be erased from Jill's mind. Surely she remembered this moment, this ugly comment, until the day she died in 2008. We all have opportunities that we blow, times when we say or do the wrong things, and we have to remember that it leaves a lasting mark. Although we can seek forgiveness and restoration and learn from our mistakes and begin to un-fail, there are words and deeds that cannot be forgotten. There are times when a parent speaks something that curses a child for life—something that never lets them go, that colors their world and their relationships forever.

> *Although we can learn from our mistakes and begin to un-fail, there are words and deeds that cannot be forgotten.*

In the story of Noah's drunkenness, we see the same situation. In Noah's embarrassment and worst moment, he lashed out at his son, who had helped him build the ark, assisted with the animals, and was going to help repopulate the earth. He would have so many descendants. But because of Noah's weakness, drunkenness, and curse, this son and the generations to follow would spend a lifetime under a cloud. There would be no forgiveness. Yes, Ham did wrong. But afterward, there was only the curse.

No number of literary awards or honors could ever dull the hateful words that were carved into Jill Faulkner's mind. No time spent with his father would bring Ham and his descendants back into a right relationship with Noah.

This is a crucial lesson for us today. At some point in our lives, we will inevitably fail those we love with our words or actions. If we don't face this reality head-on, there can be deeply damaging repercussions for generations to come. We must watch what we do and say. When hurtful words seem to escape our lips before we can catch them, or we act in damaging ways before we realize it, we need to be ready to apologize. We need to be ready to "un-fail," to redeem ourselves and the people we hurt by actively working toward change and preventing those slip-ups from influencing the lives of countless other people. Otherwise, our failure can turn into the failure and regret of many others.

THE BLESSED

We are offered some encouragement on the other side of Noah's story. The older brothers, Shem and Japheth, received blessings for their loyalty, respect, and faithfulness. They led blessed lives, and the Messiah ultimately came from the line of Shem.

Just as our words can bring pain and suffering, they can also bring life and goodness. They can encourage and bolster, lifting others into better lives.

As surely as his father's drunkenness gave Ham an opportunity to act poorly, it also created a situation in which Noah could see the honorable actions of his other sons. It gave them an opportunity to do right.

It is easy for us to choose the way of Ham, to ridicule and mock rather than to respect and aid. But the story of Shem and Japheth's faithfulness to Noah can be an example to us all that, on the other side of failure, there can be honor and fruitfulness.

It is our job to make sure our words have integrity. It is our job to make sure our words mold and guide those entrusted to our care. And when we slip up, it's our job to make things right as soon as possible.

SCRIPTURE TOOLS

Your sins are telling your mouth what to say. Your words are based on clever deception. (Job 15:5 NLT)

My tongue will proclaim your righteousness, your praises all day long. (Psalm 35:28)

A small rudder makes a huge ship turn wherever the pilot chooses to go, even though the winds are strong. In the same way, the tongue is a small thing that makes grand speeches. (James 3:4–5 NLT)

Consider what a great forest is set on fire by a small spark. The tongue also is a fire, a world of evil among the parts of the body. It corrupts the whole body, sets the whole course of one's life on fire, and is itself set on fire by hell. (James 3:5–6)

But the wisdom that comes from heaven is first of all pure; then peace-loving, considerate, submissive, full of mercy and good fruit, impartial and sincere. Peacemakers who sow in peace reap a harvest of righteousness. (James 3:17–18)

REFLECTION QUESTIONS

Here are some reflection questions you might consider when evaluating and developing a life of controlling your tongue:

1. Had Noah not been drunk, the entire ugly incident with Ham might have been avoided. The curse of generations, the separation of a family, is traced back to Noah's excess. How do our own actions give others a chance to stumble?

2. In what ways are we unable to get over how we've been wronged in the past? What are steps we can take to conquer these holds that stunt our growth? How can we find help to let go?

3. Where much is given, there is also much responsibility. What do we learn from the story of Paula Deen's words?

4. Reading what William Faulkner said to his daughter—"No one remembers Shakespeare's child"—horrifies us. But do we make those same kinds of mistakes? What can we do to overcome the effects of hurting others? How can we learn from this to prevent our words from being harmful in the future?

7

CHOOSING COURAGE

(Genesis 21:1–10)

We've all done it. We had a dream, we saw God working, felt that glimmer of hope ... and then we panicked and slapped together a different plan. Or we gave up because there was no way that original dream was going to work out. We considered it, we stressed about it, and logistically it didn't quite make sense. Whatever our story, we've all seen it, and we've all fallen victim to it. At some point, every one of us has lacked the faith that God would come through.

But when God is behind us, who can be against us? What greater purpose could we possibly have that God couldn't help us shoulder and pave the way for our success? We constantly fail to recognize that He can see much further than we can and has taken every aspect of our lives into account already.

As we stare over that precipice of fear and uncertainty, it's helpful to remember who God is. He is capable and powerful and wise. He is a God who makes promises and keeps them. We just need the courage to hand over our dreams, goals, and plans and follow through.

THE STORY OF ABRAHAM AND SARAH

Abram had lived a long life with his wife Sarai, but much to their chagrin, the couple had remained childless. One night, in Abram's very old age, the word of the Lord came to him in a vision, promising great rewards. But Abram had trouble seeing it. Where would those blessings go? Who would be there to enjoy them? Brashly, he asked God how it was possible that he would be blessed when he didn't have any heirs to receive such blessing. (See Genesis 15:1–3.)

This was a bold move, a half rebuke and half taunt from Abram to the God of the universe.

God's gentle response to this challenge was beautifully artistic. The Lord took Abram outside and said, "Look up at the sky and count the stars, if you can!" It was a stunning night, and Abram looked from horizon to horizon. The stars were limitless. The Lord said, "Your offspring will be the same."

And get this: right then, Abram believed God. And the Lord *"credited it to him as righteousness"* (Genesis 15:6). All was well…

Until the very next chapter in Genesis when Abram forgot God's promise and listened to his wife. Sarai wanted a family. She knew she was well past childbearing age, so she hatched a plan. "Abram," Sarai said, "the Lord has kept me from having any children. I want you to go sleep with my Egyptian slave, Hagar, so that I can build a family through her."

It would have been the perfect opportunity for Abram to take a stand and tell his wife that they would wait on the Lord. It was a chance to claim God's promise, an opportunity for faithfulness, for God had *promised* him descendants. All they had to do was trust and wait. But what did Abram do? Exactly what his wife requested: he slept with Hagar. And through the slave, a son was conceived.

Once Hagar realized she was pregnant, she began to despise Sarai and the plan she'd concocted for heirs, and her actions showed it. Sarai confronted Abram about the situation, but he merely said, *"Your slave is in your hands. … Do with her whatever you think best"* (Genesis 16:6). Having his permission, Sarai began to mistreat Hagar so badly that the slave ran off. Understandably, Hagar had had enough.

An angel of the Lord spoke to Hagar as she huddled in the desert, telling her that if she returned and submitted to Sarai, her descendants would increase *"so much that they will be too numerous to count"* (Genesis 16:10). So Hagar returned and gave birth to Ishmael.

After some time, the Lord appeared to Abram again and gave him a new name and a new covenant. "You will be the father of many nations, and your name will be Abraham." God also renamed Sarai, calling her Sarah. A name change is a huge deal in Scripture. God had big plans for these two and He was about to unveil just how big: He promised to give Abraham a son by Sarah so that Sarah would also be the mother of nations.

Scripture notes that Abraham actually *fell down laughing.* God promised him something so incredible, so farfetched, that Abraham thought it was a joke. He was a hundred years old, and Sarah was ninety! It must have seemed impossible. Abraham laughed. Sarah laughed. But none of that changed the fact that Sarah was already pregnant and that the Lord was true to His word. God established a covenant through the boy Isaac who was, indeed, born to Sarah the next year.

GOD WILL COME THROUGH

A central question in these passages comes from God Himself: *"Is anything too hard for the LORD?"* (Genesis 18:14). Abraham laughed but God didn't. God was at work. He was nation-building, preparing the way for many peoples, many tribes. There was nothing too hard for Him, nothing He couldn't make happen.

If only we could always remember that. For Abraham, Sarah, and Hagar, so much pain could have been prevented if they'd trusted God from the beginning. They decided to take their story into their own hands because Sarah didn't trust that God would come through. She thought she had to force some heirs into existence; she assumed she had to get crafty. God had something so much better planned for her than what she created for herself, and that's true for our lives as well. God has a better plan for us than we can devise on our own.

> *God has so much more than we could ever dare to ask. We only need to trust in Him and then wait for Him to fulfill His promises.*

No matter what, God has the resources to follow through with His promises. He has so much more than we could ever dream, than we could ever dare to ask. We only need the courage to trust in Him and then wait for Him to fulfill His promises. Too often, we take matters into our own hands, thinking we are sufficient, thinking we've got it all figured out, when God's ways are so much better and brighter. But our faith can fortify or diminish the faith of those around us. Our trust and response to God—including the times we've failed to trust Him the first time around—can bring people into the work He is doing or push them away.

Abraham and Sarah did eventually have a child in their old age. But Abraham's lack of faith caused trouble.

First, in the midst of all that happened, Hagar ended up feeling disconnected from the group she knew. This was a family she had served for many years, and then she found herself pregnant by her master and mistreated by his wife. Hagar had done exactly what she had been instructed to do, yet she ended up feeling shunned. Her only friend in this situation turned out to be God. He was there to meet her in the desert, cradle her in His arms, and give her a new, better story. God promised Hagar that her descendants would be as fruitful as Abraham's. Through this narrative, we see the lineage of two peoples: the Jews and the Arabs, descendants of Isaac and Ishmael.

The second problem came about because Sarah was angry with Abraham for doing the very thing she had asked him to do. She made a choice and then she didn't like the results. How often do we commit that same offense? We think life isn't going where we want, so we try to push our way through at our own expense—and probably someone else's too—and it doesn't turn out like we hoped it would.

There are consequences when we do not trust God. Still, He is faithful to keep His promises. Today, the descendants of Abraham are too numerous to count.

Wouldn't it have been easier to trust Him from the beginning? This is a recurring theme when we see the failures of biblical characters. It's human nature to lack faith when faced with uncertainty, and it affects each of God's followers, no matter how firm their faith seems to be otherwise. Yet there comes a time when we have to choose courage and press forward with God's plan, even if we're unsure. That is what sets a faithful servant apart.

There comes a time when we have to choose courage and press forward with God's plan, even if we're unsure.

GOD PUT TO THE TEST

In Judges 6, an angel of the Lord appeared to Gideon to tell him God was sending him to save Israel out of Midian's hand. But Gideon's response was, "But how can I save Israel? My clan is the weakest in the tribe of Manasseh, and I am the least in my family." Gideon didn't believe he was capable—and even if he was, he didn't believe God would keep His promise to be with him so that Gideon would *strike down all the Midianites, leaving none alive*" (Judges 6:16).

Gideon ended up asking for three separate proofs that it was really God talking to him and that God would really do what He said. He had to triple check God Himself in order to finally commit to what was being asked of him! Meanwhile, the Israelites were impoverished and dying.

The Israelites were crying out to the Lord as Gideon was laying down fleece on two separate nights, checking to see whether it and the ground around it was dry or wet as God had specifically promised him. Who knows what greater devastation happened that God did not intend while Gideon faltered in his uncertainty.

God knows we're never going to be as courageous as we need to be, but the beautiful reality is that God is always with us. If we are simply faithful, God compensates for our inadequacies. When we're faced with that deciding moment, we need to choose courage and take a step of faith, choosing to know that God will come through for us.

THAT FIRST STEP

Craig Groeschel is the founding pastor of one of the country's largest congregations, Life.Church. Their ministry started in Edmond, Oklahoma, and has grown to redefine many aspects of how modern ministry is done.

Groeschel began as a Methodist pastor but soon found a different calling in his life. He launched Life.Church, its numbers grew rapidly, and the ministry team sought God in their expansion. Then one weekend, after he preached on a Saturday night, Groeschel's wife went into labor. It was decided in the moment that instead of having another pastor fill in on Sunday morning, the tech team would simply play Groeschel's sermon from the night before.

A funny thing happened. God moved in that room even though Craig's sermon was merely a recording. It didn't matter that the pastor wasn't physically present in the room. God's spirit moved anyway. This was a major revelation for the vibrant young team. Life.Church was one of the first churches to have a multisite model, and this gave the team the idea of showing a video of Groeschel's sermon at the other campuses. Overnight, Life.Church became a leader in this movement. Eventually, technology caught up with the system they were running, and today a live feed of the pastor's sermon is seen simultaneously at their numerous campuses.

In an anniversary service, Groeschel shared a story from during that in-between time, when the team was still figuring out what was viable and what was possible. Once the ministry team realized that the multi-campus model worked—with the pastor's teaching on video in every service, regardless of the location—Groeschel dared to start dreaming. He came up with what he called his BHAG or Big Hairy Audacious Goal: Life.Church would keep multiplying their campus locations until they had one hundred sites!

At the time, the megachurch had just opened a handful of campuses. It was incredibly impressive to see such coordination and cooperation evolving into something that God was obviously blessing. But Groeschel was hesitant to share such a large dream. One hundred campus locations sounded like such a huge leap. He decided to share his vision with his mentor to see what he thought of such a lofty goal. The mentor merely shook his head and said, "You young people ... always thinking so small."

Craig Groeschel chose courage. He chose to follow the plan that God seemed to have set before him. At the time of this writing, forty-five locations are listed on the Life.Church website, and its Bible app is one of the most popular apps in the country. God is blessing the efforts of Craig Groeschel and his team. And God shows no signs of slowing down.

Eventually, Groeschel, Abraham, Sarah, Hagar, and Gideon were all able to let go of their concerns, let go of the uncertainties and the trivial details, and find the courage to trust in God's plan. How much smoother would our lives be if we simply put our trust in Him to begin with? If we took that first step of courage immediately instead of drawing it out? Imagine what great things would happen if we all trusted God sooner and implicitly.

Because God knows what He's doing.

CHOOSE COURAGE

There may also be times when it doesn't feel like our choices matter. Like Hagar, we feel pressed up against a wall, out of options. But there are always options for how we respond to a situation. Even if we can't choose our involvement, we can still choose to have courage to trust God or not, and that choice is made in how we respond to our circumstances.

The Lion in Winter is a great classic film from 1968.[21] Set in AD 1183, it is the tale of King Henry II and his three sons. They all want to inherit the throne, but King Henry II won't commit to a choice. The boys and his wife, played by the amazing Katharine Hepburn, variously plot to force a decision.

At a crucial point, the sons are all locked in a dungeon. Henry decides that none of the princes is worthy to inherit his throne and he would rather have other sons with his mistress so a suitable heir can be raised up. The problem he is facing is that his current sons will always be a threat. The king knows that he may have to kill them.

While locked in the dungeon, the three sons await their fate. They know they are a threat to the king; they know what he is planning to do. They hear footsteps approaching, presumably Henry II coming to kill them at last. And then we see a very interesting exchange between two of the brothers.

Prince Richard defiantly says, "He's here. He'll get no satisfaction out of me. He isn't going to see me beg."

His brother, Prince Geoffrey, laughs. He replies, "You chivalric fool—as if the way one fell down mattered."

Prince Richard then shares a profound truth. "When the fall is all there is, it matters."

We can turn to God and choose to trust Him, or we can elect a path of distrust and try to forge a way on our own.

There will be times in life where we find ourselves out of choices. Perhaps we failed to trust God and we are just now realizing the ramifications. Perhaps it is circumstances that are entirely out of our hands. While

---

21. *The Lion in Winter*, directed by Anthony Harvey (1968; AVCO Embassy Pictures).

there is nothing that we can do to change the course of what is happening, even in these moments, we have choices to make. We can turn to God and choose to trust Him, or we can elect a path of distrust and try to forge a way on our own.

A lack of faith can be our downfall, but it doesn't have to be the end. How we handle ourselves means a great deal. Our actions speak volumes, and we have an opportunity to model Christ-like behavior for others even in the worst situations. Having grace and courage under fire might be the only choice remaining, but it is a choice that is worth making.

TO TRULY TRUST IN GOD

Like the sands on the beach and the stars in the sky, God's gifts and graces are limitless. His storehouse overflows with good things He wants to share with us, His children. Can we do better than Abraham and Sarah? Or do we laugh at God's promises and go about our routines? It takes courage and faith to truly trust in God. Sometimes it takes the *greatest* courage to wait upon the Lord and trust in what He's capable of. But letting go of our fear and choosing to trust Him is how we step into un-failing. We have to start by acknowledging that God knows what He's doing and decide to trust in *His* plan rather than our own.

> *To step into un-failing, we must acknowledge that God knows what He's doing and decide to trust in His plan rather than our own.*

Even if we've already messed it up, even if it's our third or fourth chance to turn to God and hand over our doubts and reservations, we can still move onto the path of un-failing and be more willing to trust fully and readily the next time around.

What dreams do you have sitting on a shelf because you aren't certain He'll help you make them work? What greater purpose has been beating in your heart, waiting to be let out, while you slowly double-check all the logistics and continue to put off pursuing it? What step of courage and faith do you need to take in order to live the life you imagined for yourself? What goals have you laughed off, like Sarah and Abraham? God has all the resources you need. He knows all the variables and has taken them into account. Choose courage. God is waiting for you to catch up.

SCRIPTURE TOOLS

Now if you will obey me and keep my covenant, you will be my own special treasure from among all the peoples on earth; for all the earth belongs to me. (Exodus 19:5 NLT)

Know therefore that the LORD your God is God; he is the faithful God, keeping his covenant of love to a thousand generations of those who love him and keep his commandments. (Deuteronomy 7:9)

[God] will protect his faithful ones, but the wicked will disappear in darkness. No one will succeed by strength alone. (1 Samuel 2:9 NLT)

Give thanks to the LORD, for he is good; his love endures forever. (1 Chronicles 16:34)

But know that the LORD has set apart the godly for himself; the LORD hears when I call to him. (Psalm 4:3 ESV)

Surely your goodness and unfailing love will pursue me all the days of my life, and I will live in the house of the LORD forever. (Psalm 23:6 NLT)

Let love and faithfulness never leave you; bind them around your neck, write them on the tablet of your heart. (Proverbs 3:3)

REFLECTION QUESTIONS

Here are some reflection questions you might consider when evaluating and developing a life of faithful courage:

1. What are some examples of faithfulness in your own life? Who has shown faithfulness to you? Can you understand how God feels when we are faithful to Him?

2. Imagine being Sarah's age and being told you were going to have a child. Would your first instinct be to laugh? Imagine a pastor telling you he dreamed of having one hundred sites for his church. Would that make you roll your eyes? What evidence can you find in your own circle of friends and family pointing to God moving in unexpected ways?

3. When you have few choices—like in the story of the king's sons from *The Lion in Winter*—the way you choose to fall really does matter. In those situations, it might be all that you have left, the only choice you can truly decide for yourself. Have you ever been in situations where your options for handling adversity were limited? How did you fare? In what ways would you like to face struggles more strongly? How specifically can you ask God to guide you in this?

4. Is there anything that is too hard for God?

8

CLINGING TO WHAT MATTERS

(Genesis 25, 27)

Ifyou've ever found yourself horribly disappointed in your circumstances, you're not alone. It's been a theme for thousands of years. Human beings have often been in situations where they want or believe they deserve more. (Even the Little Mermaid sang an iconic song on this topic.) But what becomes important as we start grasping beyond our current situation is *what* we cling to and *why* we're doing what we do.

Do you find yourself fighting your situation primarily for your own power and prestige or because you believe it's God's plan for you? Are your efforts focused on you alone or is what you're aiming for good for the community around you as well? Because this might not only spell the difference between supported success and solitary defeat, but also whether you're still on track with Christ.

> *We're defined by the motivations that propel us into action and whether we use that tenacity for good.*

We are not defined by the circumstances we're born into. Instead, we're defined by the motivations that propel us into action and whether we use that tenacity for good. Not everyone will get it right every time. The destruction of misuse can be bleak, but the power of using it well can change the direction of history.

THE STORY OF JACOB AND ESAU

Twins are fascinating. As a society, we marvel at their similarities and differences whenever we encounter either identical or fraternal twins. Jacob and Esau, the first twins mentioned in the Bible, were alike in some ways, but their differences truly defined who they were and each one's path in life.

Jacob was an inside kind of guy. His mother taught him how to cook, and he was her favorite. Esau was an outdoorsman who hunted; he was his father's favorite. The twins fought from the start, even in the womb. Their mother, Isaac's wife Rebekah, was so concerned that she took this matter to the Lord. God answered, *"Two nations are in your womb … one people will be stronger than the other, and the older will serve the younger"* (Genesis 25:23).

Esau was born first, but his brother Jacob's hand came out in the delivery, grasping Esau's heel, refusing to be second without a fight. In Hebrew, *Jacob* means "he takes by the heel," and Jacob would indeed spend the rest of his life grabbing for the things he wanted.

A turning point in both their lives came when they were grown. Esau returned home tired and hungry after a long day outdoors, looking for game. He could smell the tantalizing aroma of the lentil stew that his twin was cooking. Esau said to Jacob, *"Quick, let me have some of that red stew! I'm famished!"* (Genesis 25:30).

Jacob, however, had a plan. He'd spent the morning cooking and pondering his options while his brother was out hunting. Jacob knew Esau would be starving, so he decided he would feed his brother … for a price. Instead of simply handing Esau a bowl, he offered stew in exchange for his birthright.

Doesn't this just sound like brothers? Jacob was asking a pretty hefty price for a bowl of stew. For context, a birthright was an honor bestowed on the oldest son, giving him a double portion of the father's inheritance. It was a big deal, and it was certainly worth much more than a banquet, much less one evening's dinner. It sounds like a silly prank between siblings, but the crazy part of the story is that Esau agreed!

Some have suggested that Esau suffered from low blood sugar and desperately *needed* to eat. It's also possible Esau thought he had little to lose. We sometimes wonder if Jacob was an amazing cook, and the lentil stew was just *that* good. Whatever the backstory, Esau's response was, *"Look, I am about to die. … What good is the birthright to me?"* (Genesis 25:32). And just like that, Esau gave his birthright to his younger brother. He gave in to his temporal needs and surrendered his God-given blessing to Jacob.

Like any younger brother, Jacob made him swear to it. (Pinky swear, perhaps.) Esau followed through, giving away his birthright, and then Jacob gave him bread and stew, undoubtedly pleased with himself. Esau ate, drank, and left.

Years passed and the twins grew further apart. When their father Isaac was an old man and could no longer see, he called for his eldest son. Esau went to him: "I'm here." Isaac said to him, "I'm old and don't have much time left. I want you to do something for me. Go hunting and prepare some tasty game for me to eat so that I may give you my blessing before I die." (See Genesis 27:1–4.)

Rebekah, the boys' mother, was listening. Once Esau left to hunt and was out of sight, she went straight to Jacob. She told her favorite son what she'd heard and instructed him to kill two choice goats. She was going to prepare a meal exactly the way Isaac wanted. She told Jacob to take the meal to Isaac himself, pretending to be Esau, "*so that he may give you his blessing before he dies*" (Genesis 27:10).

Jacob pulled on some of Esau's clothes. His mom wrapped hairy goatskins on his hands and neck to simulate Esau's hairy body. Then Jacob took the meal to his father and lied to him:

> *I am Esau your firstborn. I have done as you told me. Please sit up and eat some of my game, so that you may give me your blessing.*
>
> (Genesis 27:19)

Though very old, Isaac wasn't easily fooled. He asked Jacob, "How did you hunt and find the game so quickly, my son?"

"The Lord gave me success," Jacob replied.

Isaac wasn't buying it. "Come to me," he said, "so that I can touch you and know that you really are my son Esau."

Imagine Jacob at that moment. He's in the middle of this act, this con. He still has Esau by the heel symbolically; he's still trying to be the firstborn. And yet here's Isaac, his father, who could at any moment give the blessing and grant Jacob everything he wants. But Isaac, still unconvinced, questions him again. "You sound like Jacob."

If it were a scene in a movie, dramatic music would be building. There would be a pause as the camera closed in on Jacob's apprehensive face. Then, it would turn to show Isaac reaching slowly to feel Jacob's arm.

His old hands brush across the goatskins of Jacob's costume and Isaac says, "But your hands are the hands of Esau." The tension reaches a fever pitch. Isaac asks, "*Are you really my son Esau?*" (Genesis 27:24).

And Jacob replies, "I am."

Isaac ate the food and drank the wine. "Come here, my son, and kiss me," he said. Jacob kissed his father. Isaac smelled the clothes Jacob wore— Esau's. Isaac declared, "*Ah, the smell of my son is like the smell of a field that the* LORD *has blessed"* (Genesis 27:27). With that final piece of information seemingly in place, seemingly adequate, Isaac then gave his blessing.

Almost immediately after Jacob left his father's side, Esau returned from hunting. He cooked up a hearty meal and brought it to Isaac, requesting his father's blessing. Isaac couldn't believe what he was hearing. He shook violently, saying, "Who was it that I blessed before?"

Esau, too, was furious. He knew immediately what had happened, what his deceitful brother had done. He cried, "Bless me, too, my father!" But the damage had already been done. Jacob had stolen it.

"He took my birthright first and now has taken my blessing!" exclaimed Esau. And it was true. Isaac had made Jacob lord over Esau and all his relatives and servants. There was nothing to be done. His word had been given. The die was cast.

We can picture Esau, this time in a closeup, speaking like Michael Corleone from *The Godfather*. *"I will soon be mourning my father's death. Then I will kill my brother, Jacob"* (Genesis 27:41 NLT).

Jacob got word of this and immediately fled.

DOING THE HARD THINGS

Jacob used some pretty unsavory tactics to get ahead, and yet Scripture emphasizes Esau's choice to sell his birthright as the greater wrong. Jacob would not have been able to get the birthright had Esau not chosen to give it away. Esau might have been a great hunter and sportsman, but he certainly was not a very strong, forward-thinking leader.

Regardless of Jacob's deceit, he was still chosen to carry on the covenant of Abraham. And Esau, who chose his physical desires over his spiritual blessings, was excluded from the lineage of the Messiah.

It's a confusing lesson for us. On one hand, it shows the humanness and brokenness of these Bible characters. They really are no different than us! They are prone to deceit, selfishness, and manipulation. But it also shows the importance of clinging to what really matters, like a birthright, even if it means denying our physical desires and wants. It shows the impact of decisions that pull us away from God's direction.

Was Esau really worthy of his birthright if he was so easily persuaded to give it away? It's an important question. We are not sure if Jacob was the better man, but he certainly was the stronger. Jacob always wanted to be the leader, always grabbed at his brother's heel. And he did end up being the more ambitious son. Not in physical terms or by the standards of the world, but Jacob was strongest through his determination, his spirit, and the way he pushed for more instead of settling for what he was given.

The story of Jacob and Esau illustrates the importance of clinging to what really matters, even if it means denying our physical desires and wants.

It is also important to note that as her sons grew older, Rebekah chose to favor Jacob. This was no accident. He was smarter and conniving; he had to get that from somewhere! His mother had seen the outcome of the lentil soup episode and recognized its significance. Obviously, Esau's willingness to give up his birthright for a mere bowl of soup was a very good indication of the kind of decisions he would make someday. It showed that while he may have had bodily strength, his mental fortitude and determination were lacking. She must have wondered how Esau could possibly make good decisions for the whole family if he so easily made poor ones for himself. What would their future look like with him as their leader when Isaac died?

Rebekah recognized that life isn't just about how many animals one could kill or even the position you're born into. It is about perspective and sound judgment. Rebekah saw that Jacob would be the one to stick it out and do the hard things necessary for leading a clan.

BUILDING FOR OTHERS

After some years had passed, while on his way back home, Jacob had an extraordinary encounter. He met God. But he didn't just meet God; the Bible says Jacob *wrestled* with God! Imagine the tenacity and brazenness!

And rather than destroying Jacob (as He certainly could've done), God chose to spare him. He engaged Jacob in his own game. Then God changed Jacob's name to Israel, indicating the significance of the event. God knew that kind of strength and bravery could be a good thing. It was that very spirit that God was looking for to ensure the lineage of Christ.

> *Jacob's strength and bravery demonstrated the kind of spirit that God was looking for to ensure the lineage of Christ.*

The tale of Jacob is fascinating, as it almost seems to turn our expectations of what God would want on its head. Rebellion? Lying? Fighting with God? Refusing to accept the path we were given? Not the themes we're usually celebrating. And it gets even more interesting when Jacob has his own children. He, too, had a favorite son—Joseph—who caused conflict. Remember when Joseph's brothers got angry about Joseph's colorful new threads and his dreams? (See Genesis 37.) They got tired of the youngest brother consuming all of their father's attention, so they did what any good brothers would do: they threw Joseph into a pit and then sold him into slavery. However, that harsh treatment launched Joseph on a life in which he was able to save his brothers and thousands of others by storing up food in Egypt for the famine. When they say God works in mysterious ways, they aren't kidding.

> *When used for empty, worldly success, our tenacity, stubbornness, and self-confidence create confusion and failure.*

But there's a catch. Our tenacity, stubbornness, and self-confidence—when used for empty, worldly success—create confusion and failure. Acting merely for our own gain, when we know it's wrong and might hurt other people, is not the right way to go about things. We can do a lot of damage when we do things for ourselves at the detriment of others. Just look at what's happening in the U.S. right now with the billionaire class—we have severe homelessness, starving children who can't afford school lunches, and countless people dying rather than putting their families in debt to see a doctor while the wealthy minority are gathering up every cent they can. That is not what God's prized tenacity is about.

And this is where it gets tricky. These traits are useful when they're used for God and His plan in our lives. When those traits are used for God's glory, they have limitless potential. When you stick to your walk with Jesus even when times get hard. When you keep being there for your community despite people telling you it's not worth it. When you keep showing up for a friend no one else cares about. When you keep loving others despite them not returning the favor. When you do these things, it makes an astounding difference in reshaping our communities and bringing light to people's lives.

Susan B. Anthony grew up in a Quaker household, readily accepting and living by the belief that everyone is equal under God. After years of teaching, then fighting for an end to slavery, Anthony met Cady Stanton in 1851. Together, they fought for women's rights in earnest. They traveled around the country, demanding women's right to vote through public speeches and supporting their work by cofounding the American Equal Rights Association and writing articles about women's equality for its associated paper, *The Revolution*.

When the fourteenth and fifteenth amendments passed, guaranteeing all men the right to vote regardless of ethnicity or prior slave status, the two women were furious. Yes, they were glad that the country had accomplished something great in recognizing black men and giving them a voice, but women were still barred from having a legitimate say in government and society. This pushed both Stanton and Anthony to form the National Woman Suffrage Association to try to change the Constitution yet again.

Over the years, Anthony voted anyway and was subsequently arrested, tried, and fined. She led a major protest, helped to unite and merge suffrage associations, and gave speeches, including the well-remembered "Declaration of Rights," written by Stanton and fellow suffragist and writer Matilda Joslyn Gage. Susan B. Anthony spent over fifty years spreading the idea that women deserved equal rights and pushing for those rights. And she never got to see women earn the right to vote. She died in 1906, fourteen years before the nineteenth amendment finally passed in 1920, giving women a right that Anthony fought for much of her adult life.[22]

Yes, there was the visible spread of ideas, but Anthony faced a lot of pushback and hatred for her efforts. She had to hold fast to what she believed women deserved in order to keep going. She wasn't doing it for just herself. She was doing it for the many women who would be affected by her actions, by her tenacity, in the future. Anthony is known today as one of the primary leaders of the women's suffrage movement. Thanks in large part to her efforts, women in the US have voted, served in government, and helped to change policy for over a hundred years now.

Tenacity is so important when it's used to build. In Jacob's case, it built a nation.

THE UNLIKELY UNCHOSEN

Stories of power always seem to fascinate us. We love to turn to history, particularly World War II, for examples. A most interesting period is seen in England leading up to the war. King Edward VIII wished to marry a divorced American socialite. But as head of the Church of England, King Edward was forbidden to marry a divorced woman if her ex-spouse was still alive. So Edward declared his love and abdicated the throne in December 1936. His brother Albert became George VI and served as king throughout World War II.

The moving story of Albert's challenge and determination can be seen in the movie *The King's Speech*.[23] It's a mesmerizing tale of a man who never wanted to be king, who always knew his brother would be king. And then, the crown was thrust upon him quite unexpectedly. It was an utterly different scenario than the story of Jacob and Esau, but with similarly important consequences.

Albert had a severe stuttering problem, but as king, he would have to be able to communicate effectively with his people. He needed the crown

22. Nancy Hayward, ed., "Susan B. Anthony (1820-1906)," National Women's History Museum, www.womenshistory.org/education-resources/biographies/susan-b-anthony.
23. *The King's Speech*, directed by Tom Hooper (2010; Paramount Pictures).

to appear strong in the face of adversity. Albert showed amazing tenacity. With the help of a speech teacher, he worked to overcome his speaking difficulties and was able to inspire his country amid turmoil and despair. Historical triumphs just don't get any better than this.

But there's more to the story. After abdicating the throne, Albert's elder bother Edward did not go quietly into the night with his new bride. Recently declassified historical archives show that Edward visited Germany during the war to conspire with Adolf Hitler. The two were planning the future of England after the war. Footage and photos show Edward giving full Nazi salutes. It is also said that Edward assumed the Nazis would crush the Americans, doing nothing to stop it. Even though the British people didn't want him as their king, Edward still fully intended to return as their leader once Hitler was victorious. There are even claims that Edward leaked Allied war plans.

Imagine what might have happened had Edward remained on the throne. England most likely would have taken an entirely different direction in the war. The country might have had a king who dragged them into something they didn't want. History would have turned out very differently.

Through it all, as in the story of Jacob and Esau, we see the younger, unchosen brother rise up to lead with strength, when the older brother would likely have bumbled or harmed his people. The whole world owes a great debt to Albert, King George VI, who guided his country through the horrific time of war, without compromising his morals for personal power or gain.

A CAREFUL GRIP

We have to make sure we're hanging on to the right things. When we grip our original ideas too hard and don't leave our hearts open for God and other people to speak into our lives, we can end up fighting battles that don't even make sense, closing our hearts to the possibilities around us and leading us far off course.

Hirō Onoda fought as a second lieutenant in the Imperial Japanese Army during World War II. Sent to defend Lubang Island in the

Philippines, Onoda's service is fairly unremarkable except for one amazing fact: Onoda did not surrender until 1974, twenty-nine years after the war was over.

> *If we cling to the wrong things and close our hearts off to God and others, we can end up fighting battles that don't make sense.*

Onoda was sent to hamper Allied attacks on the island and was given orders to never surrender or take his own life. Onoda heard of the Japanese defeat as early as October 1945 from a leaflet dropped on the island, but he believed the information was Allied propaganda. His orders had been clear: surrender was not an option. Onoda continued to patrol and wreak havoc on the inhabitants of the island for three decades. He burned rice collected by the farmers and even killed several people. Local police attempted to apprehend Onoda over the years, both by force and by persuasion. Police dropped off family photos and letters that begged Onoda to believe that the war had been lost so long ago. Again, Onoda believed it was all a lie. He simply could not accept the facts.

Armed with a rifle, five hundred rounds of ammunition, a sword, a dagger, and several hand grenades, Onoda was able to hold out for twenty-nine long years. He refused to believe that the battle had been lost, refused to accept that his beloved Japan had been defeated. He would not believe nor acquiesce until the Japanese government flew Onoda's former commanding officer, Major Yoshimi Taniguchi, to Lubang. Taniguchi had not been in the army for many, many years, and was now a bookseller, but on March 9, 1974, Taniguchi ordered Onoda to finally surrender to the Philippine police.

This story is terribly sad. Spending all those years fighting a battle that was already over was a tragic waste. Yet that is where so many people find themselves today. They're holding on to a mistaken belief, idea, or assumption that benefits no one or that God has already taken care of. In these situations, release would be better for everybody.

Are you holding on to old ideas, old emotions, or old conflicts that you should give over to God?

All of us continue to fight on what Gloria Gaither called "battlefields of our own making." Consider what old ideas, old emotions, or old conflicts you might still be clinging to. Are those really the battles you should be fighting? Whether they're within your own heart or between you and other people in your life, take some time to reflect on what might have changed as you've grown in God. Maybe you're still lingering over something that you should give over to God.

Relief and freedom can be found on the other side of the battle, but we will never arrive there until we lay down our weapons and choose to believe that Jesus can handle it and we are safe in His arms. We can waste years of our lives making decisions based on fear, a misunderstanding, a lack of knowledge, or a minor conflict because we are afraid of what happens when we let go. The war has already been won. God will catch us and bring us into a place of greater understanding. We simply must believe. Then we will have the energy and strength to be tenacious about the things that *do* matter and will make a difference, the things that are part of God's plan for us.

WHO ARE WE FOLLOWING?

Throughout history, men and women have used their ambition for evil. But many have also used it for good. People have overcome challenges and adversity through determination and faith. When this is paired with a heart for God and a desire to follow Jesus, incredible things happen.

This is possible for you as well. Focusing entirely on your own needs won't get you very far as a spouse, sibling, employee, leader, or follower of Christ. But coupled with a desire to grab the heel of those who have gone before you with Jesus-focused self-denial is exactly what the world needs from you.

When God seems slow to move or when His direction goes against what we want or think is possible, it can be easy to go our own way. To make our own path. These decisions might lead to worldly satisfaction or success, but at what price? Like Lieutenant Onoda, they also might lead us in circles, never moving forward in our lives because we're too set in our beliefs to really look around us.

> *As Christians, we must decide if we are truly following Jesus or our own thoughts and desires.*

As Christians, we must decide if we are truly following Jesus or our own thoughts and desires. Very few of us will get it right every time. But that's the beauty of the cross. Just like Jacob, we stumble along the way, but if we allow Jesus to work through us, He will transform our selfish mistakes and show us how to un-fail and use those mistakes for good, stepping out boldly in the way that He has for us—not the way we have for ourselves.

Jacob made many mistakes, but his heart was to follow God, and he was relentless in that quest. May we have that same tenacity paired with hearts that are softened to God's leading.

SCRIPTURE TOOLS

I do not run like someone running aimlessly; I do not fight like a boxer beating the air. No, I strike a blow to my body and make it my slave so that after I have preached to others, I myself will not be disqualified for the prize. (1 Corinthians 9:26–27)

Since we are surrounded by so great a cloud of witnesses, let us also lay aside every weight, and sin which clings so closely, and let us run with endurance the race that is set before us. (Hebrews 12:1 ESV)

"Restrain your voice from weeping and your eyes from tears, for your work will be rewarded," declares the LORD.   (Jeremiah 31:16)

Endurance produces character, and character produces hope.
(Romans 5:4 ESV)

Rather, as servants of God we commend ourselves in every way: in great endurance; in troubles, hardships and distresses.
(2 Corinthians 6:4)

Pursue righteousness, godliness, faith, love, endurance and gentleness.
(1 Timothy 6:11)

If you suffer for doing good and you endure it, this is commendable before God. To this you were called, because Christ suffered for you, leaving you an example, that you should follow in his steps.
(1 Peter 2:20–21)

REFLECTION QUESTIONS

Here are some reflection questions you might consider when evaluating and developing a life of godly tenacity:

1. Who should we cheer for in the biblical story of Jacob and Esau? Jacob stole a blessing, but Esau flippantly threw his birthright away. Who was the stronger and why?

2. What kind of leader do you think Esau would've been had Jacob not stolen his blessing?

3. Jacob wrestled with God, and God ended up blessing Jacob. What does this tell us about the nature of God?

4. Godly tenacity can take us on incredible adventures, as it allows us to achieve great things through Him. What individuals do you know personally who exhibit this determination and strength, and how do you see God working through their adversity?

5. Sometimes it's hard to lift up those we disagree with, but God instructs us to pray for our leaders regardless. How does this relate to the encounters we examined with Jacob and Esau?

SECTION THREE:
AN UN-FAILING
PERSPECTIVE

Truly un-failing, truly changing, means shifting our perspective to see our lives through God's eyes and follow our true purpose in Christ. But looking at the world and our circumstances with new eyes can be hard. Processing our past, present, and future in a new light takes determination and a bunch of self-reflection.

We believe you can do it.

Here's the catch: you will still make mistakes. But we encourage you to understand that you will keep making mistakes in your efforts to live a changed life. We encourage you to plunge in with everything you have and try to see things differently, try to see the world the way God sees it. It's the only way through. Have the faith to try, to attempt, to reach the other side.

The Gospels are rich with lessons from Peter. Besides Jesus, he is the only person recorded as having walked on water. It is easy to miss the great takeaway from this miracle when viewed and taught in a way that focuses on Peter's *failure*. Yes, he sank. Pastors often point out that his faith was not as strong as it should have been. Peter took his eyes off Christ and look what happened!

It is true that Peter stepped out on the water and then began to sink. He had to rely on Christ for rescue. He started strong and ended weak. What embarrassment. What failure…

But let's not miss what really did happen: Peter walked on water. *He walked on water!* What a remarkable feat. If Peter's faith had been so small, if he'd refused to believe that anything new could happen, he never would've stepped out of the boat to begin with. He started seeing the possibilities of the world with Jesus. Peter didn't hesitate either. He didn't wait and talk himself out of this crazy idea. Peter saw Christ and simply had to be with Him. Jesus said, "Come on," so Peter went.

Imagine being one of the other men in the boat. We think it's safe to assume that any of them could have risen, stepped out over the side, and walked to Christ. They could have participated in the miracle. They could have been in the company of the Savior. Instead, seeing Peter start to sink, they all decided to stay in their seats.

The church is quick to pounce on bold people like Peter who make mistakes. It is easy to point a finger and think poorly of those who lose their way or fall hard. It's easy to cite their stumbles and falls as evidence of their lack of faith and devotion. But how often is our inactivity an indictment of our own faith deficiency? Do we sometimes reassure ourselves that *we're* doing just fine because "at least we're not sinking"? Do we completely ignore the fact that we tend to stay safely in our own little boats, missing out on miracles that are there for the taking? How many times have we missed tremendous growth, blessings, conversions, or miracles in life because we chose to remain where it was more comfortable? How many times have we stayed blind to something because we refused to see? Or missed out on a relationship with someone because of our judgmental tendencies?

Approaching the circumstances in our lives in a new way, with fresh eyes and hope, can be daunting. It can be scary. We might end up taking a couple steps back for every few steps forward. We might find ourselves feeling like we're out on open water, by ourselves, trying to reach Jesus. But this is the only way we get to see the world anew. It is only way we can live in the fullness of all that God has for us.

Sometimes the other side of sinking can be a pretty remarkable place. Ask Peter. He was wet and a little shaken, but he'd seen the amazing love and generosity of Jesus in a unique way. He saw the world in a new light, and it only happened because he took the risk and believed, briefly, that he could do it. Let's start approaching our lives with new perspectives, seeing its circumstances, its opportunities, and its people through God's eyes. Let's take the leap and step out of the boat, even if we don't feel ready yet.

9

EMBRACING GROWTH

(Numbers 20:2–13)

If you find yourself struggling as you try to force old methods onto new problems, you're not alone. Sometimes it feels like we just figured out how to handle one thing and then something new pops up. Sometimes we've used the same solution for years, and it doesn't quite seem to be clicking when we use it again for the fifteenth time. Even when we know better, we still resort back to what we knew. Whether we're tired, frustrated, or just plain scared, we snap back into our go-to response and repeat our efforts, doing the same thing over and over and wondering why what worked before isn't helping us now. We ignore that still, small voice that's telling us we might need to (gasp!) try something new.

Unfortunately, life is not going to keep giving us the same problems that require the same solutions. Even if it looks like it's the same problem, we still might need a new solution. What we did for that one issue when we were twenty-one might require a new response now that we're forty-four. As we mature, how we approach life's problems changes. And as we're making these decisions, we need to consider what is driving our choices. Are we choosing to respond this way because it's easy? Because we're feeling lazy? Because we're simply crossing our fingers and hoping it will work? When we refuse to open ourselves up to growth, it becomes easy to find ourselves failing over and over.

> *When we refuse to open ourselves up to growth,*
> *it becomes easy to find ourselves failing over and over.*

On the other side of that coin, are our decisions aligned with what we believe God wants for us? Are we listening? If not, are we ready to be courageous and double down and truly listen to Him? We may not always get it right, but it is always better to know that at least we genuinely tried. God is rooting for us; we just need to keep that realization in mind.

When it comes down to it, it's about being in a spot and a mindset where God can use us, where we are ready to grow.

THE STORY OF MOSES

When thinking of failures in the Bible, we rarely talk about Moses. It's easy to visualize Jonah running from the Lord or Peter denying Christ those three painful times or Judas counting his silver. But Moses? The great leader? His failures are harder to see. This is why it's important to explore them if we are to fully understand the heart of God and His willingness to use broken vessels.

Moses had great strength and leadership capabilities. He led God's people out of Egypt in one of the most captivating stories found in the Bible. The Hebrews had been enslaved for so long. Their bondage was a tough, brutal affair that only ended after terrible plagues broke the will of the mighty Pharaoh. It's a great story, and it's been portrayed on the silver screen numerous times, most memorably in Cecil B. DeMille's classic, *The Ten Commandments*.[24] We can see Charlton Heston lifting that rod high above his head while the Hollywood special effects gurus of long ago create walls of water so the Israelites could safely cross the dry riverbed. That scene embodies all the strength and drama that old Hollywood loved to portray. Moses was *the man*! He was God's man, the Old Testament hero brought to us in glorious Technicolor.

> *Moses failed in large and small ways—just like the rest of us. But that didn't stop God from using him.*

And yet Moses failed in large and small ways—just like the rest of us.

That didn't stop God from using him. God changed the world through Moses despite his imperfections and failures. But if we are to see Moses clearly—and understand fully the triumphs of his successes—then we must learn from the broken areas of his life. And there is one point in Scripture where Moses got it so wrong that it cost him dearly.

The account is found in the book of Numbers. Now, Numbers is not one of the most popular books in the Bible; it's not the kind of book that we usually tell new Christians to read. But it is filled with all kinds of wonderful information and stories that can speak loudly to us today.

Let's start with the story's setting: It is hot. Everyone is milling around in the desert. There have been deaths and significant heartache. Miriam, Moses's sister, has passed. The people of Israel are stuck with no water and a thirst for change. They feel misled. Things were better when they were slaves in Egypt, where they had grain and figs, grapes and pomegranates. An angry mob forms before Moses and his brother Aaron, shouting, "Why have you brought us all into this desert to die?! Why have you taken us to this evil place without food, without water?! What were you thinking?"

---

24. *The Ten Commandments*, directed by Cecil B. DeMille (1956; Paramount Pictures).

This was all too much for Moses to bear. He had risked so much to do what God had commanded. He had stepped forward bravely even though he didn't feel like a leader, didn't *want* to be in charge of the great exodus from Egypt. But God chose him to conduct the largest jailbreak ever recorded. And now it had come to this. Revolt. The people were blaming Moses for their unhappiness, and he could do nothing but steal away from the assembly and fall face down at the entrance of the meeting tent.

Yet even in this hour, humbling himself before God, Moses was still a leader. Aaron had his brother's back, so he also fell face down before the tent. Although the going had been rough, Aaron continued to follow Moses, continued to believe in him. They had seen it all together. They had stood before the powerful, they had passed through parted waters, and they had rejoiced in God's deliverance. Now, as the storms were gathering, Aaron still chose to follow his brother.

God honored Moses and Aaron by showing His glory. The Lord said, "Moses, you and Aaron take the staff and assemble the people. Make sure you have their attention. Then while you're standing before them, command the rock over there to provide water. While the people watch, water will come out of the rock. You will give them enough cool water to drink to satisfy every single one of them and their animals too."

It would be nice if this story ended with the brothers doing as they were commanded, but that's not what happened. Moses did take the staff as the Lord commanded, and the assembly gathered before the rock. And then it happened. Maybe he was annoyed by all the complaints, maybe he felt the people needed an extra reminder to keep themselves in line, maybe he didn't feel confident in just talking to an inanimate object, or maybe it was just too much overall and his anger simply got the better of him. Whatever the reason, Moses turned toward the people and yelled at them.

"Listen, you rebels!" he cried. "Must we bring you water from this rock?" Then, instead of commanding the rock, as God told him to do, Moses raised his staff up high and brought it crashing down upon the stone. Then he did it again.

Surely the flair and intensity of the moment caught the crowd's attention, but Moses hadn't obeyed God. Instead of commanding the rock, Moses had hit it, twice.

Thankfully, instead of punishing everyone for the unfaithfulness of Moses, God allowed the water to flow for the people anyway, so they could drink. Even when Moses was angry at the *rebels* and then rebelled himself, God still provided, and the water still flowed. He was not going to forsake His children and His promise to them. The Israelites confronted the Lord with chaos, and He showed faithfulness.

> *Instead of punishing everyone for Moses's unfaithfulness, God allowed the water to flow so the people could drink.*

But just as God produces water for us to drink, disobedience produces consequences. "*The* Lord *said to Moses and Aaron, 'Because you did not trust me enough to demonstrate my holiness to the people of Israel, you will not lead them into the land I am giving them!'*" (Numbers 20:12 NLT).

Getting to the promised land was and is a big deal. Not only is this true in the Bible, but it is a theme found in literature and culture around the world. We all want to arrive, to be firmly established, to find success. It's a powerful concept. But in this passage, we learn that Moses would never be able to finish what God had started with him.

It's important to note that this occurred after everything Moses had already done and accomplished. He'd trusted God over and over—he was no stranger to the ways of the Lord. Yet he failed to follow God's explicit instructions during this ordeal and forfeited his future.

The story is bothersome.

Moses stood up to Pharaoh and was there for the ten plagues, speaking out for God's enslaved people. He parted the Red Sea and moved tens of thousands of people through the desert and out of harm's way. Then, after one mistake, God rewrites Moses's role. Cuts him off from seeing the dream he's followed for years come to fruition. It seems unfair, doesn't it? Wrong even. But it's not that simple.

What seems like a one-time blunder was the last in a series of mistakes that Moses made, including:

+ He killed an Egyptian and fled. (See Exodus 2:11–12.)

+ He failed to circumcise his son. (See Exodus 4:24–26.)

+ He broke the original tablets with the Ten Commandments that were engraved by God. (See Exodus 32:19.)

God had told Moses to use his staff to strike a rock to obtain water prior to this. (See Exodus 17:6.) And there were numerous times in Scripture where Moses was told to use his staff to initiate God's miracles. This time, however, God had changed it up. "You don't need to strike the rock this time," we can imagine God saying. "Just speak to it. That way, you will show the people a different side of My power. We're separating the power from your staff."

But Moses did a couple of things wrong besides striking the rock instead of speaking to it. He yelled at God's people, calling them rebels. Then he had the audacity to say, *"Must we bring you water out of this rock?"* (Numbers 20:10), implying that he and Aaron caused the water to flow, not God.

Do you see the complexity of the situation? This wasn't a matter of God getting angry at a one-time offense. This was God pointing out that Moses was going through the motions. He wasn't truly listening anymore; he made a choice, separate from God's instructions, and because of that, Moses had undermined God's lesson for His people—a people who struggled with their faith, with their belief in God's power.

> *How many times do we struggle with what God is saying to us and do the same things that we've always done?*

How many times do we as Christ followers get into difficult situations and struggle with what God is saying to us? How many times do we revert to the same old things that we've always done because that's how we've always done it?

What makes this more painful was that Moses had been given a special dispensation of grace. The previous generation had already been told, "You're not going to the promised land" because of their lack of faith, but God had made an exception for Moses. He allowed Moses to live and make the journey—an opportunity that Moses then lost at the rock. We can almost hear God say, "Look, Moses, you are suffering from the same things that everyone else is suffering from. You have accomplished so much, but in order to go into the promised land, I need a people who will listen to Me."

Moses needed to be a good follower as well as a good leader. He needed to be ready to do what God asked of him, even if it was something new. This meant listening to God instead of assuming he knew what should happen or using one of God's miracles to make his own point. Later, Moses pleaded with God to allow him to enter the promised land, but God became angry and said, "*That is enough. … Do not speak to me anymore about this matter*" (Deuteronomy 3:26).

SOMETHING NEW IN STORE

This is such an important lesson: God has something new in store for you. His storehouse is abundant. His mercies are boundless. God has a wealth of resources to aid you in dealing with the troubles of your life. He has a plan and a purpose and a destination for your life—but He is not going to ask you to use the same tools that you've been using from the time you were a spiritual infant. As you mature in your faith, so do God's expectations and offerings. God expects you to grow, to keep your ears open and listen. As we mature, we are held to a higher standard. We know better.

Paul talks a lot about this in 1 Corinthians and Philippians. He states that as we grow up in our faith, God gives us more opportunities to see His majesty and His power. He wants our lives to become a witness to those around us, to draw others to Him.

Ultimately, it is not just about us. It's not just about striking the rock. It's about being in right relationship, the right communion with God, and following where He leads. We are not meant to just take hold of that new thing; we must allow it to become the compass and engine that drives us forward into the future. An old preacher might put it this way: "I want to get a fresh word from the Lord!" God always has a fresh direction for us when we need it most. We need to listen and obey.

> *God always has a fresh direction for us when we need it most. We need to listen and obey.*

When Moses failed to follow God's instructions, there were greater repercussions for both him and the people of Israel beyond prohibiting Moses from entering the promised land. By striking the rock instead of speaking to it, Moses prevented all of Israel from seeing the new thing that God was doing. He prevented a deeper relationship between God and His people. The Israelites didn't get to see this new display of power that would have enhanced their faith and reassured their hearts.

Here's something not to miss, though—and this is important. What happened when Moses did strike the rock despite God's explicit instructions? Did God refuse to let the water flow just to prove His point? Did He call Moses out in front of everyone? No. Water came out. God wasn't going to keep the water from the people; He didn't want them to die of thirst.

This wasn't about the water. God could have provided water in any way He wanted. This was about God's people—His children—and an opportunity to show them something new, to reveal more of Himself and deepen their belief in Him.

The greatest lie ever told by the adversary is that the God of this universe doesn't want you to have what you need in order to become all that He has in store for you. The truth is that the Israelites were not going to starve or thirst to death. Even if Moses had rolled the rock down a hill instead of striking it, God wasn't going to abandon His people. This idea that God only provides when we act a certain way is a lie. He always provides. God will always meet us in our need.

But God has so much more for us than mere daily provision. He offers a relationship that can deepen only when we listen and obey.

We see the same kind of situation when we read John 21. After the resurrection, the disciples returned to fishing. They spent three rewarding years with the Master Teacher but immediately went back to striking the same rocks, the same as they'd always done. They went back to what they knew!

What did Jesus do when He returned to them after being resurrected? Did He say, "I've had enough of you" or "You all failed"? No. Christ met them on the shore of the Sea of Galilee one more time. He found them fishing but He didn't leave them there.

God was done with Moses striking rocks to obtain water. He was ready to move on, to take Moses somewhere else in their relationship and for that relationship to change all of Israel. He needed Moses to do something else, to be more. He needed Moses to be a different kind of follower and leader. He needed Moses to grow.

In a similar way, when God met the disciples at the shore, He was in essence telling them, "Okay, we're going to start this journey one more time … but no more fishing. I have something more in store for you."

NO LONGER STRIKING ROCKS

God has more in store for us too, even in our brokenness, even if we've struck the same rock repeatedly for years, or even if we watched everyone else do it the same way our whole lives. But we must meet Him where He's asking and be ready to step forward in a new way. It's how our communities will see deep change.

During our time at Christ Church Memphis, we had some pretty unique experiences when we tried new things, when we took new steps of faith. One of those faith steps was hosting a television program called *We Believe in Memphis*. The city of Memphis has its share of troubles, but through this talk show, we offered hope by presenting guests and ministries that had a positive impact on the region. We met dozens and dozens of amazing leaders making a difference.

One such encounter was a particular blessing. Imagine our joy in meeting with a lawyer who was part of the group representing Martin Luther King Jr. during the sanitation workers' strike in Memphis in 1968. It was right after speaking to the workers that the civil rights leader was killed. In our city. Memphis will always bear the burden of being the location of Dr. King's assassination.

We were so excited to meet this attorney, and he lived up to the hype. He was a delightful man and told of being with Dr. King at Mason Temple the night before he was killed, when Dr. King gave his famous "I've Been to the Mountaintop" speech. We asked the lawyer, "Tell us what it was like to be in that place. What was it like to hear him say those words?"

The lawyer told us something that has stayed with us: "People have to remember that Martin Luther King Jr. was a very human, very fragile man. We've made him into something superhuman. He wasn't superhuman. He had flaws; he had broken places. But there was something inside of him, and I saw it that night, where God had moved him up a level in the conversation about justice."

When he was making his mountaintop speech,
Martin Luther King Jr. wasn't striking rocks any longer.
He was listening to the possibilities.

As we reflected on human weaknesses, human failures and fragility, a thought came to us from the Holy Spirit: at that point, when he was making that mountaintop speech, Martin Luther King Jr. wasn't striking rocks any longer. When King gave that speech, he said, "I may not get there with you, but I want you to know tonight that we as a people will get to the promised land." He said this in such a way that there seemed to be something speaking through him. You can watch him give this speech online; it is striking to realize that he would be killed shortly afterward. It was as if he knew of his impending death but chose to step forward anyway—he knew there was something greater out there, something more out there for everyone. He was listening to the possibilities.

Friend, no matter what you may think of Dr. King, you have to be in awe of the fact that there were those who have stood in the gap for justice and righteousness. They did so time and time again. They did it for more than just themselves. They knew that the only way to transform our communities was to stop striking the rock and instead start talking about the possibilities.

In Dr. King's letter from a Birmingham jail in 1963, he wrote, "I am less worried about the Ku Klux Klan and the White Citizens Council than I am about the white Protestant church who are more concerned with order over justice."

STARTING SMALL

Reading about someone as influential as Dr. King might make us want to shuffle back into our corners again, where we hope God is asking less of us, asking for something we can handle. But remember, God is giving us what we need to succeed, and He is directing a path for us that will get us there. We may start with striking the rock and that's okay, so long as we eventually move on from it.

There was an art teacher who once tried to teach an older gentleman how to paint. He had never picked up a brush, so to him, the whole experience was pretty foreign. It was awkward dipping into the paint, applying the pigment to the canvas, and trying to make shapes and colors into something beautiful.

In that same class, a little girl was sitting and painting beside the older gentleman. She looked at his work and said, "Oh, that is so pretty." He took this as code for, "Wow, that is really bad." He stared at his painting, discomfort creeping in as he continued swiping his brush across his work, trying to focus, to turn it into something better.

Still staring at the canvas, the girl asked innocently, "What are you painting?"

"What do you mean?" the man thought, somewhat affronted. "Can't you tell it's a house and a tree?!"

He took a deep breath and said, "I'm painting a story of what happened when I had an important conversation near an oak tree. It was a very special time in my life." He gave an affirmative nod of his head, but he was beginning to question what he was doing in the class. Was he wasting his time here?

"Oh," the little girl replied, "well, then it's beautiful to you, and that's all that matters."

Possibly noticing the tension of the interaction, or the frustrated look in the man's eyes, the art teacher paused. She told the older gentleman, "You would be surprised at the number of adults who have never painted in their life who come in and sit down thinking that when they start to paint, they should be Picasso or Monet." She smiled kindly at him. "I always remind them that everyone has to start out somewhere small."

We will not always get it right, but as long as we are seeking to go deeper, to mature, to grow in our faith, that is all God asks!

Most times, we are called to start out small. We are called to bloom where we are planted, to tend to what we are given, to grow, to learn, to follow. We will not always get it right, but as long as we are seeking to go deeper, to mature, to grow in our faith, that is all God asks! He wants us to listen and be prepared for Him to do a new work.

If you are still striking the rock, then start there.

If you're on your way to the promised land, start there.

If you hear God say something new, start there.

Just know that nothing about God is predictable or routine. Know that He has something more in store for you.

READY TO GROW

The truth is, just like everybody else, Moses started at the beginning, in the place where God could use him. He couldn't even speak that well when he started his journey and was afraid to do so in front of others. It is not a coincidence, then, that God said at the pivotal moment, "Moses, I want you, not Aaron. I want you to speak to that rock so that the people will know something amazing has happened."

And Moses didn't do it.

We feel sorry for Moses, but the lesson is for us too. We continue to do the things that are easy enough and ready enough and available enough. We strike the rock. Again and again. We find contentment because despite our disobedience and our reluctance to trust God and grow, He still provides water where we are. Yes, God continues to bring water. But know this: God doesn't simply want to give us a cup of water. He wants to quench our thirst.

> *God doesn't simply want to give us a cup of water.*
> *He wants to quench our thirst.*

It's not a coincidence that eight hundred years after Moses, Jesus sat next to a well with a woman who had been doing the same thing over and over again. Jesus said, "Aren't you tired of striking that rock? For sitting next to you is living water." (See John 4.)

Imagine sitting next to Christ, who is offering to take care of your thirst for good.

Our churches need us to stop revisiting the same places, the same gaps, and the same brokenness with the same answers and platitudes. Our state, our country, and our world need us to stop striking the rock. We need to speak to that rock and to all those things that are inhibiting who we have been called to be. Then we need to step into that space and let God use us, even if we have failed in the past. Even if we get it wrong the first time. Even if our brokenness tells us we aren't capable. God is capable. He will guide us on our path of un-failing.

There are no coincidences in Scripture. Jesus is known as the *Logos*—the Word in Greek—that Word spoken into eternity, from whom all things come. If God can speak that Word to bring the stars into existence or part the waters from the land ... if He can speak that Word and create night and day, morning and evening, then He can speak that Word into your life. He can speak to the rocks in the church's life and the rocks in your community's life, and you can know that water will flow. Not just any water, Jesus says. Living water. And you'll never be thirsty again.

Are you tired of striking the same old rocks? God has met you in your journey, but maybe it's time to trust Him on where the next steps will lead. Maybe you need to follow Him onto the road of un-failing. Maybe you need to trust His leading in your marriage, in your relationships, in your job, in your involvement in your community. Maybe you're ready to go to the next level and want to be shown the way. Maybe your heart has been pulling at you about a certain topic, but you haven't felt ready to leap in and help. Or maybe you're at a place where you're just thirsty. You're parched in the dusty desert. Jesus offers you living water today, water that will change your life forever. Stop striking the rock. Start listening and get ready to grow.

SCRIPTURE TOOLS

Hezekiah trusted in the LORD, *the God of Israel. There was no one like him among all the kings of Judah, either before him or after him.*
(2 Kings 18:5)

Jehoshaphat stood and said, "Listen to me, Judah and every inhabitant of Jerusalem! Trust the LORD *your God, and you will stand firm; trust his prophets and succeed!"* (2 Chronicles 20:20 CEB)

Those who put their trust in the LORD, *who pay no attention to the proud or to those who follow lies, are truly happy!* (Psalm 40:4 CEB)

Trust in the LORD *with all your heart and lean not on your own understanding.* (Proverbs 3:5)

God is indeed my salvation; I will trust and won't be afraid. Yah, the
LORD, *is my strength and my shield; he has become my salvation.*
(Isaiah 12:2 CEB)

Blessed are those who trust in the LORD *and have made the* LORD *their
hope and confidence.* (Jeremiah 17:7 NLT)

Thus said the Lord GOD, *the Holy One of Israel, "In returning and rest
you shall be saved; in quietness and in trust shall be your strength."*
(Isaiah 30:15 ESV)

REFLECTION QUESTIONS

*Here are some reflection questions you might consider when evaluating
and developing a life of expectations based on God's goodness and storehouse of
blessings:*

1. Being responsible for a large group of people anywhere is a chal-
    lenge. Moses found it difficult, especially after years in the desert.
    What would have prevented Moses from trusting God and doing
    exactly as instructed?

2. Why is it so important to seek God's guidance? What dangers
    await if we don't seek the Lord? What examples in history do we
    find when this occurred?

3. To receive something new, we sometimes must do something new.
    God wanted Moses to stretch himself, but Moses chose to follow
    the same paths as before. Why is it so easy to do what we've always
    done rather than seeking out the new that God has in store for
    us? How can we better equip ourselves to be prepared for new
    journeys?

4. God was angry with Moses for not following His instructions, yet God provided water for His people anyway. What does this say about the nature of God? How does this speak to you personally?

5. Moses could not speak well, so his brother Aaron communicated for him. Yet at the time when God wanted Moses to do something new, God commanded Moses to do the speaking himself. In what ways do you feel unequipped to handle tasks God has given you? What can you do to open yourself to listening to God's instructions? Why do you think God wanted Moses to use his own voice?

10

REDEFINING SUCCESS

(Mark 10:35–45)

Society can push us to keep wanting more—to be higher up, richer, more influential, powerful, or famous. But that's not what we were made for; it's not what we are meant to focus on. When we fail to keep our eyes on what God wants for us, we can find ourselves pushing for a kind of success that may sound good in theory but can be wiped out in a flash. The kind of success that has us working toward all the wrong things and straying further from God's hope and plan for us.

As time passes, we may find ourselves trapped in the rat race or the comparison game, further from God than we've ever felt. The good news is that He is always there to guide us back toward Him and remind us what we *were* made for.

THE STORY OF JAMES AND JOHN

The largest religious movement in all the world began with only twelve men.

Jesus chose only a dozen to disciple and pour into day after day. And these men weren't plucked from lofty roles in society. Matthew was a tax collector. Philip and Judas were some sort of tradesmen. Simon the Canaanite was only known as a zealot; perhaps he was a community organizer. Not all of their occupations are known, but five to seven of the dozen were mere fishermen, James and John among them.

James and John, the two sons of Zebedee, were businessmen, entrepreneurial in their dealings. When Jesus called them out for ministry, they were tending the nets with their father. They were able to do this easier work because they had hired other men to do the dirty work, such as preparing fish for market. James and John were successful and strategic thinkers, always looking to get ahead.

It should come as no surprise that the two brothers approached Jesus one day about the pecking order of the disciples. As men who had led and managed others, they knew a little something about what it meant to be in charge. Having an edge, a little bit of power, was important to these two.

"Teacher," they said, "we want you to do us a favor."

(Mark 10:35 NLT)

It's interesting that they start out with the deferential title of authority. Perhaps it was an attempt at flattery.

Picture Jesus turning to face the pair. "And what do you want Me to do for you?" We imagine there might have been a twinkle in Jesus's eyes as He faced them. He already knew what was coming.

The brothers eagerly replied, *"Let one of us sit at your right and the other at your left in your glory"* (Mark 10:37). They automatically went for the best seats in the house. Clearly, there was a power mindset with these two.

They waited intently for Jesus to respond.

"You don't even know what you are asking," Jesus said to them. "Can you drink from the cup I am going to drink from or be baptized with the same baptism as Me?"

"We can!" they answered without hesitation.

Jesus looked at them. "You will drink the cup I drink and be baptized with the same baptism as Me, but awarding places at My right hand or My left is not for Me to give."

Their disappointment was clear. This wasn't going as they'd hoped.

Gently, Jesus said, "Those spots belong to those for whom they've been prepared."

Unfortunately for the brothers, someone overheard the conversation and told the rest of the disciples. They were angry, to say the least. How dare James and John try to wiggle their way into positions of power behind everyone's backs! Jesus heard their indignation and called all of His followers together for a meeting. There was a misunderstanding that needed to be cleared up.

"You know how the rulers of this world, the people who are in charge, hold it over their subordinates?" Jesus asked them all. "They rule with an iron hand. You see how they flaunt their authority, hand out decrees, and tell people what to do?" The disciples all agreed. Even James and John.

"We aren't like that," Jesus said. "We do things differently. *You* will do things differently. We look at the heart, not the status or success of a person."

Jesus loved these men, and He took His time looking at each of them. This was a big concept that He was communicating. It was the core of who Jesus was and what His kingdom was about. It was imperative for them to understand.

It was imperative for Jesus's disciples to understand that whoever wants to become great must serve others.

He continued gently but firmly, *"Whoever wants to become great among you must be your servant"* (Mark 10:43).

The silence in the group must have been deafening. This was not what they knew. Wasn't Jesus building a kingdom? Weren't they going to throw off the yoke of the Romans? Yes, Jesus had exemplified this practice many times over, but for everyone to do it, to serve in order to become great? That turned common sense on its head. This thought was so counterintuitive to the world and how it operated. It was a hard thing to understand. But there was more.

Jesus added, *"And whoever wants to be first must be slave of all"* (verse 44).

A slave! What had become of the talk about Jesus and His kingdom on earth? Wasn't He going to be the King of Kings? Wasn't He going to reign? Was He really saying that they must lower themselves, giving up what little power they might have achieved by following Jesus in the first place?

Jesus was delivering a hard lesson, but it was truly at the core of what would be demanded of His followers. He said, "Even the Son of Man didn't come to be served but to serve."

There it was in a nutshell. It was a gentle but perfectly clear rebuke of James and John. But it also struck a chord with the other men, who were indignant over the brothers' request. And as His words hung in the air, Jesus foreshadowed His death for the fourth time in just a matter of days: "I came to give My life as a ransom for many."

SERVING WITH OUR LIVES

This wasn't just a failure of James and John; all of the disciples failed to understand what Jesus was really about. They were all looking forward to being part of the *kingdom*. They believed Jesus would soon rule. They all thought they were working toward something slightly different than He had planned for them. The disciples became riled up because they were all on that path; they all misunderstood. It's not that they didn't love Jesus— they did—but they still desired power. They wanted it enough that they were overlooking what Jesus had been trying to show them, what it meant to truly follow Him.

The failure of this encounter boils down to our desire for power, for a certain kind of success. John and James asked Jesus for the opposite of what He probably would have liked to see happening in their hearts. These two men knew about power. They had experienced power as businessmen, and they wanted more of it. Their lust for it, to be part of those at the top, can be seen leading them further away from Jesus, and His calling for them, in three ways.

First, their desire for power distracted them from being faithful to their calling—to follow Jesus, learn from Him, and be His disciples, teaching His ways and showing His love to the world. They're not being great disciples if they're missing one of His main points because they're too focused on advancing themselves.

This desire to be promoted caused them to lose sight of the vision Jesus was sharing with the group. Jesus was all about empowering His followers to step into what God had for them. His approach had nothing to do with organizational hierarchy. It was about what to do next, where to go next, who to serve, and what was coming. The two brothers disregarded the call to bloom where they were, and they sought to advance within the group by asking for preferential treatment. They were distracted by the desire to move up among the twelve disciples, and something simple like this is all that the adversary needs to keep God's kingdom from being built here on earth! If we focus on the wrong things, then the right things won't ever be accomplished, and we might never know how badly we missed the mark. We might never realize the potential joy we squandered while chasing after or being distracted by things that Jesus hasn't called us to.

If we focus on the wrong things, then the right things won't ever be accomplished, and we might never realize the potential joy we squandered.

The second issue caused by James and John seeking power was the relational problems it caused. The others heard what the brothers were attempting, and they were angry. Imagine giving up the life you knew—your friends, family, career, and former dreams—to follow Jesus and live by His call of equality and service, while a few of your friends are trying to position themselves over you behind your back!

When our focus is distracted, relationships are challenged. When we only consider ourselves, relationships end up strained or feeling impossible, and what God is doing is all about relationships.

Jesus was bringing these twelve men together to change the course of the world. They were all valuable members of His team, but James and John made the others feel less valued. Instead of trying to secure their future positions at the top, the brothers should have spent more time following the example of Christ—and this is exactly what Jesus brought to everyone's attention. It's not about who is in charge or who has the best seat, Christ points out. It's about serving. And this mindset can change everything, from our daily interactions to our entire purpose in life.

The third thing we notice is that James and John were spending their time on unnecessary considerations. What did it matter who sat beside Jesus? What ultimate difference would it make to the overall success of what Jesus was trying to impart and accomplish?

We see this so often in the political arena when both sides argue about the minutia of what someone said instead of focusing on providing food for the hungry and jobs for the needy. We see fights over semantics and tabloid drama while people are lacking and hurting. We see partisan divides when what we need is unity to pass much-needed legislation. Truly, we all spend time on unnecessary things. We all fall prey to the distractions and our own selfish motivations. This was summed up with a powerful meme online that read, "If I found out that I had one day to live, I would party like there was no tomorrow ... Jesus found out the same news and spent His last day washing the feet of others." It is so important to put our own pride and desires aside to be faithful followers of Christ.

Our job as Christ followers is to serve and disciple others so that they, too, will rise up and do the same.

That goes for all of us. Not just James and John. All of the disciples and all of us. Our job as Christ followers is to serve and disciple others so that they, too, will rise up and do the same. This was the lesson that Christ was trying to teach. He was clear. Christians are to lead by putting themselves last. We are to lose it all—status, achievement, pride, success—and in the process of doing that, we will find it all. That is true success. But to start working toward that, to start un-failing, we must redefine our idea of what it means to be successful in our lives here on earth.

The cup that Jesus would drink would be a harsh death on Golgotha. This path would lead the other disciples to the same type of end. Eight of the apostles would die as martyrs and two would be crucified. When Jesus said, *"Take up your cross, and follow me"* (Matthew 16:24 NLT), it was not just a figure of speech. This was no rehearsal. It was the real thing. Jesus wanted these men to know the truth. He wanted these brothers to know that it wasn't about who was in charge or where someone sat. It was about serving others with their lives.

And following Christ is still the same for each of us today.

Our reward for our life's work is not of this world. It doesn't happen now. It is eternal. Though some get to enjoy those fruits during their earthly existence, for most of us, it seems only the struggle remains. We do the hard work but might fail to enjoy what becomes of it in our lives here and now. Yet God's Word says a heavenly house with many rooms is being prepared for us. His love overflows with abundance. Our actions in this life will be reflected in that place. While we're here on earth, the more intentionally we seek Him, the more we will each find our own hearts strangely warmed. We will find comfort and purpose in our actions, even if we don't find traditional success. And sometimes, we find success when we commit to being true to following God and what we believe in.

FOR LOVE OR MONEY

In the middle of the many struggles we face in our lives, focusing on what really matters can often be what saves us and brings us success both now and in the future with Christ.

Chip and Joanna Gaines were the hosts of the popular *Fixer Upper* show on the Home and Garden Network.[25] They grew their television personalities into a whole industry of renovation, innovation, and design. However, things did not begin well for the amiable hosts.

Chip was a struggling contractor who loved his wife, but Chip knew he was destined for more than what life had offered the couple so far. Through many failed schemes and plans, the Gaines family was, in some ways, at wit's end. They were rich in love, but their financial situation was precarious. Chip knew he needed to make money to give Joanna the life he thought she wanted. Then along came a television opportunity. A producer and camera crew followed the young couple around for some time, filming a "sizzle reel" for what they hoped would turn into a reality television program of some sort.

There was a problem, though. The producer was not impressed with what he was seeing. Yes, the young couple from Texas had plenty of charm. Yes, they looked great on the screen ... but something was missing. They were trying hard to be television stars rather than simply being themselves—and it wasn't working. The crew knew that if they didn't quickly find that special element that would set them apart, that spark that would make them uniquely watchable, then the show would not happen.

It was just then that another of Chip's schemes reached a messy ending. Somehow, Chip had purchased a houseboat, sight unseen. He planned to remodel the boat for the family to live in while they got back on their feet. The boat arrived as the television crew was there filming the last bit of footage.

While the cameras rolled, an interesting dynamic was captured. The boat was a wreck. Chip had spent their money on a craft that didn't even look seaworthy, let alone suitable for the couple and their young children to inhabit. The cameras continued to capture Chip's dismay and Joanna's slow realization of what had happened. It was a disaster, but the couple didn't scream or fight. The two came to terms with a horrible situation while showing their love for one another, despite the disappointment. It was a colossal failure any way one might choose to look at it. Chip tried to comfort Joanna, and Joanna tried to steady herself to make the best of this

---

25. *Fixer Upper*. Produced by Michael Matsumoto. HGTV, 2013–2018.

nightmare purchase. The money was gone. The couple had no choice but to make it work.

That's when the television magic happened. It was not during the times when the couple were happily trying to perform. It wasn't when all was well. The whole *Fixer Upper* show was born through Chip's huge failure of buying a disgusting boat and nearly losing everything.

> *By showing their true character in the face of adversity, Chip and Joanna Gaines experienced un-failing.*

The un-failing was the couple showing their true character in the face of adversity, focusing on what really mattered, despite the surprises and hardship. The un-failing was engaging footage of a young couple coming together with grace and humor to salvage a bad situation. The un-failing was a network buying the show. The un-failing was when Chip and Joanna Gaines acquired their whole future.

A hit television program was born. Its success revitalized their hometown of Waco, Texas. Many lives changed. Target stores launched a whole Home and Hearth line of goods designed by Chip and Joanna.

A design dynasty happened because Chip failed to consult Joanna before purchasing a boat, and they focused on what was most important. They found success in their relationship, in being there and having grace for each other. For them, it led to success in their professional lives.

We love this story! And it could have ended so badly. It could have been the quick end to the couple or led to one trying to get a show out of the failure of the other. Instead, it is the perfect example of the importance of love and service to one another over vying for a position or striving for an achievement. Chip and Joanna Gaines didn't just want the TV job—they needed it. They could have easily let that need, that desire for success, become the focus. In their desperation, they could have turned on one another when the boat came in and they realized that all was lost.

But their love for one another was more important than the lost money or the struggling sizzle video. It was more important than the idea they initially had of what success looks like and how to go about getting it. They put each other above their personal desires, needs, and goals. Joanna could have come down hard on Chip for his boat purchase, but she didn't. She was there to love, serve, and support him, just as he was there to love, serve, and support her. They were at their best when they were trying to comfort each other. It wasn't about trying to get ahead or becoming famous.

God saw their hearts. He took this *failure* and forever changed the couple's lives. They truly stumbled into His grace and blessings. When we focus on what really matters, God is able to do incredible things that would have been stunted by our own motivations, our own selfish desires. These two were successful, but not just because they created an empire. They were successful because they were able to maintain their relationship through a difficult time that transformed into something greater for them. When we focus on loving others, God can do so much more in our lives. He can help us to un-fail whatever situation we find ourselves in.

That's how He works. But we need to keep our eyes on Him and our hearts ready to serve.

LEAVING A LEGACY

Many people in leadership who have influence and potential for power simply choose to be servants to others. They volunteer their time even when it's no longer an uphill trajectory for them. Even when their positions are in jeopardy, disappearing, or rolling off to someone else, they care enough about the overall purpose to remain involved and keep at it.

Maxie Dunnam has been a leader in the world of Methodism for decades. He served as president of Asbury Theological Seminary—the Orlando campus is named after him—and he led the Upper Room organization for many years, producing programs to support the devotional lives of Christians worldwide. He met Mother Teresa and Pope John Paul II. Dunnam grew Christ Church in Memphis into a strong, vibrant congregation focused on serving the city he loves, which is how we met him. And yet with all of these accomplishments, when our team came on board at Christ Church, Dunnam chose to remain on staff to help the transition.

The church was moving on, and Dunnam knew he was headed out at some point. No one would have blamed him had he chosen to retire, but he chose to be supportive. He had done so much to help other people, so much to spread God's hope and love! And when asked to help us despite stepping down from his previous leadership role, he stepped up to that new plate and served with a smile. Now in his eighties, he still keeps a schedule that would tire men half his age. He always helps everyone do the best job they can, regardless of their position or seniority. Maxie Dunnam is a great example of someone who was given a position of leadership and used it to serve. His definition of success was helping others, even if it meant stepping aside.

What matters is our legacy—our reputation among those who knew us and the positive impact we had on their lives.

Power and position come and go. Societal success that took a lifetime to build can be wiped out in a heartbeat. Through age or circumstance, life changes. What matters is our legacy—not where we land in the hierarchy of society, but our reputation among those who knew us and the positive impact we had on their lives. We are called to make disciples. In doing so, some of us may find ourselves promoted to a corner office—but we need the perspective that working in an office with extra windows gives us a wider view of where we need to serve.

IT'S A WONDERFUL LIFE

It would be rare to find someone who isn't familiar with *It's a Wonderful Life*,[26] the classic holiday film that brings joy and encouragement each year at Christmastime. George Bailey, played by the great Jimmy Stewart, finds himself in the unusual situation of being able to see what the world would be like if he had never been born. An angel named Clarence (Henry Travers) helps George discover that the world truly is richer and better because of

---

26. *It's a Wonderful Life*, directed by Frank Capra (1946; RKO Radio Pictures).

George's presence. What seemed to George to be a life of quiet desperation is shown through a new perspective, and we find ourselves moved by the character's transformation. Each life truly does touch so many other lives.

George wanted to see the world and build skyscrapers. These were not bad ambitions. George was still a great guy who was friendly and warm to those he met. He just wanted to achieve, to be successful. He wanted to do something great. The film's theme, however, is that George's *achievement* was the contribution he made to his hometown of Bedford Falls by simply living his life and being who he was.

Most of us want to do more, to be more. We find ourselves reaching for those things that the world tells us are important. The world's definition of success is often not the same as God's, but George's story in *It's a Wonderful Life* probably came close. It is all about being a positive influence in a negative world. It's about blooming where we are planted, being an encourager and a servant. It's about one life touching other lives.

THE SUCCESS OF SERVING OTHERS

Having the best corner office or seeing your name in lights shouldn't be the end goal. Asking to sit on either side of the throne shouldn't be the game plan. God's bounty is abundant. We don't have to compete for His approval or blessing. It's right and just to celebrate and cherish when big experiences happen, so long as we remember that life is a vapor, changing quickly, here and gone. Rewards and money and positions aren't permanent. The person trying to find their worth and joy in these things will likely spend a lifetime searching for more. And the person who loves Jesus and loves like Jesus is much more likely to find, as George Bailey did, that life is wonderful already if you look at it the right way.

If you've fallen into the *failure* of living for worldly success, for power, for clout, for whatever it may be, maybe it's time to start un-failing and focusing on the difference you can make in the lives of other people. Because defining how you view success can change not just your own life, but the lives of everyone around you. Stepping into servanthood can reinvigorate your community, revitalize your relationships, and bring you closer to God and His huge heart for you, His child. If you've found yourself chasing the societal dream lately, maybe it's time to take a long hard look at your life and values and reprioritize.

We don't have to stay stuck in the rat race. We can start un-failing and recognizing new opportunities and potential pathways by redefining our perspective on success today. God has so much more planned for us than we could ever imagine.

SCRIPTURE TOOLS

Teach me your ways, O Lord, that I may live according to your truth! Grant me purity of heart, so that I may honor you.

(Psalm 86:11 NLT)

Let your eyes look straight ahead; fix your gaze directly before you.

(Proverbs 4:25)

So we fix our eyes not on what is seen, but on what is unseen, since what is seen is temporary, but what is unseen is eternal.

(2 Corinthians 4:18)

But I'm afraid that your minds might be seduced in the same way as the snake deceived Eve with his devious tricks. You might be unable to focus completely on a genuine and innocent commitment to Christ.

(2 Corinthians 11:3 CEB)

And now, dear brothers and sisters, one final thing. Fix your thoughts on what is true, and honorable, and right, and pure, and lovely, and admirable. Think about things that are excellent and worthy of praise.

(Philippians 4:8 NLT)

His purpose was to equip God's people for the work of serving and building up the body of Christ. (Ephesians 4:12 CEB)

Serve wholeheartedly, as if you were serving the Lord, not people.

(Ephesians 6:7)

REFLECTION QUESTIONS

Here are some reflection questions you might consider when evaluating and developing a life of focusing on the right things:

1. James and John knew what it was like to be in charge. Having had power, they seemed hungry for more. Their desire to be seated at Christ's right hand and left hand caused division among the apostles. Do you see any similar desire in your own life? Does this passage give you guidance in your future steps?

2. Jesus instructs us to serve others. He tells us that to become first we must be last. How does this conflict with our contemporary lives? What does this say to those of us in positions of leadership?

3. Each of us has opportunities to effect change in the world around us. To look out for others. To serve instead of jumping to the front of the line. In what ways can you do this more effectively at work? At home? In your relationships? What dangers are there in not looking or watching closely enough?

4. In the film *It's a Wonderful Life,* we see that every life touches so many other lives. What are some ways that your everyday life has touched others? What are ways that others' lives have impacted your own?

5. Chip and Joanna Gaines saw a failure become a major turning point in their lives. What makes us so scared to fail? How can we train ourselves to view *failure* as a learning experience?

11

BELIEVING ANYWAY

(John 20:24–29)

Life can look bleak sometimes. There are days when the evidence of God's presence seems to slip away entirely, and we end up feeling very much alone. We don't notice His blessings anymore, can't see His hand in our lives, and start to wonder deep down if we are on our own in this world.

These doubts can come creeping in at any moment, but they hit us hardest when our surroundings don't reflect our hopes and dreams. When the relationships break apart, the health issues hit, the career takes a nose-dive, or someone we love passes away. We try to be kind to our neighbors, to invest in our relationships, to pray, to give ... but we see nothing come of it.

Frankly, we often stop believing in God's promises. We start to turn to ourselves, to our own eyes and logic; we make assumptions based on what we *can* see in the moment. We enter a dark tunnel, leading from one upset to another. But our God is not a God of the moment. He's an eternal God who weaves together everyone's lives throughout history to set up His plan, His way. He is always there for us, even when we're struggling to see it.

> *God weaves together everyone's lives to set up His plan. He is always there for us, even when we're struggling to see it.*

We've mentioned several doubters and skeptics throughout this book, and we know how God dealt with their lack of faith. Many of them lacked faith even though they were receiving angelic messengers or direct contact with God. How do we handle a trying situation when God is not sending His angels, when it seems He's nowhere to be found?

THE STORY OF THOMAS

Jesus was a Man with a plan. His words, stories, and parables were all given to impart lessons on many levels. He was a teacher, constantly and consistently, and a good one at that. Even the steps He took had purpose—where Jesus traveled mattered.

Such was the case in the death of His friend Lazarus. (See John 11:1–44.) The disciples didn't know Lazarus had died, but Jesus knew. And He knew He could show them something important through His friend's death. It was a foreshadowing of what would happen in His own life. For their sake, so they might believe in Christ and gain some understanding of what was to come, Jesus decided to raise Lazarus from the dead.

The disciples, on the other hand, just knew that Jesus wanted to go to Judea. They were not thrilled. They'd been in Judea with Jesus before. They were afraid and said, "Rabbi, last time we were there, the Jews tried to kill You! They were going to stone You to death, and yet You want to go back?"

Jesus offered a poetic explanation. He said, *"Our friend Lazarus has fallen asleep; but I am going there to wake him up"* (John 11:11).

The disciples didn't understand. "He'll get better," they responded, thinking Jesus spoke of natural sleep, probably thinking this trip sounded like a waste of time. Now, Jesus spoke plainly, "Lazarus is dead. Let us go to him."

This is the moment that Thomas spoke up. Thomas often seemed to have a pessimistic view of things. "Sure, let's go with Jesus so that we may die right along with Him." Talk about a downer! If Thomas were a character in *Winnie-the-Pooh*, he'd absolutely be Eeyore.

Perhaps Jesus had this particular lesson of redemption, resurrection, and hope with Thomas in mind. It wasn't that Thomas was disloyal or that he was against Christ. It takes a great deal of courage to say, "Let's go die with Him." Perhaps Christ was attempting to transform the disciple's resigned attitude. Imagine the scene when Thomas finally saw Jesus call Lazarus forth from the tomb! The look on his face must've been wonderful. Where Thomas expected death, he was met with life instead.

This isn't to say that Thomas's fears were unfounded. The religious leaders really were riled up from hearing about the exploits of the prophet Jesus. Their plots against Jesus grew with every account of signs and wonders they heard. After the resurrection of Lazarus, Jesus no longer moved about publicly. He stayed with His disciples, preparing them for events soon to unfold. The disciples were still processing all the miracles and mighty acts they'd seen this Son of Man accomplish, but the fear of repercussions was surely starting to press in. Thomas was probably just trying to get a handle on Christ's encouragement, on believing Him regardless of how a situation first appeared.

Then everything changed. The nightmare arrived. Jesus was arrested, tried, and put to death. He was placed in a cold, dark tomb. It had all come to a halt. Their movement ended at Calvary. It was finished.

And yet, it wasn't.

Contrary to appearances, it wasn't over at all. After three days, Jesus rose from the tomb, triumphant in the fulfillment of all He had predicted. He presented Himself to His disciples by dramatically appearing in a locked room to be with them. And the disciples rejoiced. They were completely overjoyed. And why not? They'd been hiding, locked away and scared that they would share the same fate as their teacher. But here He was, bringing tidings of peace to them. Not to mention, He was very much alive! It was the moment when so much came together for these men, when many of Jesus's more cryptic teachings finally made sense. He had conquered death. It was a great time for the disciples. Minus Thomas.

Thomas had been suffering by himself. Misery might love company, but Thomas didn't really seem to want it. In his melancholy, he'd distanced himself from the others and therefore missed this miraculous appearance by their resurrected leader. He missed out on the in-person blast of hope.

> *In his melancholy, Thomas distanced himself from the other disciples and missed the miraculous appearance of the resurrected Jesus.*

"You should've been there, Thomas," the other disciples surely said to him. "We saw the Lord!"

"Yeah, right." Thomas was having none of it. He said, *"Unless I see the nail marks in his hands and put my finger where the nails were, and put my hand into his side, I will not believe"* (John 20:24).

Oh, Thomas! It didn't matter what his friends who were practically his brothers said. It didn't matter how ecstatic they were or how much they insisted they were telling the truth, that hope was alive and well. He wouldn't believe it unless he saw it with his own eyes, felt it with his own hands. He was adamant. No matter how hearty their testimony, Thomas would not believe.

A week went by. The disciples were still trying to figure out their next steps, still sorting out how to make sense of it all, when Jesus popped in again, suddenly appearing in the room although the doors were locked. Jesus stood miraculously before them all once more and said, "Peace be with you!"

Then, the Gospel of John tells us, without saying anything further, Jesus turned immediately to Thomas. This visit was for him.

Jesus didn't say, "Shame on you for not believing in Me!" He didn't scold Thomas. He simply said, *"Put your finger here; see my hands. Reach out your hand and put it into my side. Stop doubting and believe"* (John 20:27).

Jesus gave Thomas the opportunity to have his doubts removed. Scripture doesn't even mention Thomas touching Jesus; it just records Thomas saying, *"My Lord and my God!"* Finally. Finally, Thomas believed. It was total surrender, his choice of words proclaiming, for a Jew, his acceptance of this Jesus as total Christ and total Lord.

Jesus gently told Thomas, "You've seen Me and believed. But blessed are those who haven't seen yet still believe."

EVEN WITHOUT THE EVIDENCE

There is great compassion in this account. Thomas lost so much hope, became so depressed about the events around him, that he isolated himself from the other disciples. Have you ever been there? Where things were so hard, so seemingly hopeless, that you started shutting everyone out? Even when someone had good news, it felt impossible to accept it.

The other disciples are rejoicing, reassuring Thomas that Jesus is alive, but Thomas can't see past the hurt, past the fear. It is terrifying to step back into that place of hope and belief, to potentially have our spirits crushed all over again, but we need to step out of that mindset to reconnect with God, to make it through, to un-fail. Because staying in that zone of doubt will only hurt us in the end, cutting us off from other people and from the love that God is trying to show us.

Staying in that zone of doubt will only hurt us, cutting us off from other people and from the love that God is trying to show us.

Jesus took the time to return to the disciples again for the primary purpose of loving Thomas. He wanted Thomas to know and believe; He did not want to leave this man behind. The heart of Christ is best seen in these quiet, loving moments in which He teaches strong, and sometimes hard, lessons with intimacy, intention, and kindness. How easy it would've been to lash out at Thomas, to reprimand him for his lack of faith, but Jesus wanted to reconnect with this struggling member of the group. He went out of His way to ensure that Thomas would be redeemed and rejoin them.

There could have been a number of reasons why Thomas wanted to see Christ in order to believe. This situation, Jesus taking on the sins of everyone, dying on a cross and rising from the dead ... it had never happened before! It will never happen like this again. Despite their faith, despite Jesus's teachings, the disciples had every right to be upset, to be worried that nothing would ever be the same. And it wouldn't, but not for the reasons they probably had running through their heads in the aftermath.

Thomas may have wanted to be sure it wasn't just his buddies trying to lift him out of his depression. Or some kind of magic trick that wouldn't last. Most likely, Thomas truly wanted it to be real, something he could follow forever. His faith had been very strong in the past. Remember, it was Thomas who said they should go die with Christ. It wasn't that he didn't support Christ and believe in His message wholeheartedly. There is no evidence that this was the result of a full faith crisis. But what Thomas might have failed to realize is that sometimes we are called to continue on even when we don't have any evidence that God is with us.

Even without being an actual witness to the resurrection, Thomas could have still pressed on as a believer. He could have helped establish the church anyway. He could have continued in the things he felt God had for him. Isn't that what we are all called to do?

What we learn from Thomas is that sometimes God calls us to things that don't give any signs of earthly success. Yes, we will catch glimpses of what God is doing, but many times, those glimpses come after a long time of service. We may only see the fruits of our efforts in the lives of those we serve if we hang in there long enough—and sometimes not even then!

A GREATER PURPOSE

There will be periods in our lives when we won't see what we expected or hoped to see. The world won't align in a way that yells, "God is still here!" or "Your work has an impact!" or "This is what you were meant to be doing!" Honestly, it will almost never be that obvious. We must keep our eyes open and our hearts willing to believe that God is still there anyway or that we are making a difference, that our efforts are not in vain. In our hearts, we need to embrace the knowledge that our pressing forward matters, regardless of evidence or circumstances.

> *In our hearts, we need to embrace the knowledge that our pressing forward matters, regardless of evidence or circumstances.*

Rosalind Franklin (1920–1958) was a British chemist whose contributions to science weren't fully recognized until after her death. Francis Crick and James Watson, who were awarded the 1962 Nobel Prize in Physiology or Medicine for their groundbreaking DNA model, had based their work off of Franklin's research after her colleague shared some of it with them without her knowledge—and clearly without her consent. What was done couldn't be undone, so even after publishing her own article, the honor of discovery still fell to the men. Her contribution was a mere footnote in an article published in *Nature* magazine. After leaving King's College, Franklin left DNA behind and studied coal and viruses, helping lay the foundation for structural virology. Her earlier work is now recognized as revolutionizing the field of molecular biology. She may not have seen the credit she deserved during her lifetime, but her contributions still impact us to this day.[27]

Rosalind Franklin's work mattered enormously. Despite being overlooked and somewhat pushed around, she was instrumental in making

27. "Rosalind Franklin Biography," *A&E* Television Networks, June 15, 2020, www.biography.com/scientists/rosalind-franklin.

scientific discoveries happen even in our lives today. Thankfully, she didn't need the accolades to keep going, although she certainly deserved them!

As we noted in chapter eight, Susan B. Anthony kept fighting for women's rights for over fifty years. The amendment for women's voting rights didn't pass until after her death, but she remained steadfast her whole life. She believed she was making a difference, even if the laws didn't pass in her lifetime, even if she wouldn't be around to enjoy the fruits of her labor, even if she was hated and called a nuisance in the meantime.

Sometimes it will seem like we are on our own and the world is pressing against us. We will be unsure of how to step forward, how to keep going, as we face disbelief, ignorance, indifference, and even hostility. We must keep our eyes on what really matters. We need to believe in ourselves and what we're doing, to hold on to our purpose. It's not about the accolades; it's not just about us. We are part of something greater, and un-failing means believing and continuing with God's plan for us, even when we can't see the success, the ending, the breakthrough, or the recognition. Just because you can't see the evidence, or the result of what God is doing or what you're doing, doesn't mean it doesn't matter or isn't working or helping.

> *Un-failing means believing and continuing with God's plan for us, even when we can't see the success, the breakthrough, or the recognition.*

We simply must keep at it.

And every so often, someone will see God in us, but only if we continue to do what He is calling us to do. He calls us to be examples of His love and His promises. Even when we feel like we're failing at that, we can still find hope in the most unexpected places.

R. Brad Martin is the retired chairman and former CEO of Saks Fifth Avenue. A vibrant and intelligent leader, Martin served as CEO of Saks and its predecessor firm for nearly twenty years, during which time the company grew from ten stores based in East Tennessee into a Fortune 500 enterprise. During his tenure, the value of the company's stock increased more than twelvefold.

The terrorist attacks of September 11, 2001, occurred during his tenure. Immediately after the World Trade Center towers in New York crumbled to dust, the city was in shock. People needed signs of hope to fortify them, to help them endure. They had to look no further than the Saks windows on Fifth Avenue. Onlookers saw the windows draped in black and containing the words "With Sadness." Under Martin's leadership, the window displays changed regularly and were continually used in the aftermath of the tragedy as a stage to give positive messages to a community that so desperately needed them.

As the window displays continued, Martin received a stunning message from the priests of St. Patrick's Cathedral, located just down Fifth Avenue. The priests and staff of St. Patrick's were coming by the Saks windows seeking comfort and encouragement for themselves.

This isn't to say that the church leaders found no comfort in God during this time of crisis. It simply means that these leaders, depleted from ministering to others day after tiring day, found God afresh in the windows of Saks, of all places. When powerful circumstances threatened to push the priests into despair, the inspiration of these store windows somehow gave them strength. The priests were just people too. They had their own weaknesses. And sometimes the words of comfort to others were difficult to speak in such dark times. The store displays spoke to these servants and gave them the power to keep pressing on as they did their work at the cathedral. God used a department store chain in a special and very personal way.[28]

Trusting amid doubt and difficulties doesn't just happen. Window displays don't just appear. The Brad Martins of the world find ways to lift others up at just the right time, even when they don't know who is being helped or how. They listen with their hearts to hear what is needed.

Keep showing your hope, keeping standing in your belief that God is there. You never know who else needs to see you doing it.

---

28. Shane Stanford and R. Brad Martin, *Five Stones: Conquering Your Giants* (Nashville, TN: Abingdon Press, 2013), 71–74.

The stories of the apostle Thomas and the Saks Fifth Avenue windows also point out the necessity of community and the danger of trying to do it all on our own. We weren't made to walk in this world alone. Thomas's melancholy caused him to withdraw from the group, and it was this seclusion that made Thomas miss Christ's first appearance to the disciples. Fellowship is important. Being part of the church is vital. We are not in this thing alone, and even with our idiosyncrasies, we should always be seeking togetherness. We need others. That's why Jesus taught communion and fellowship and the concept of serving together.

> *You never know who needs to see you showing your hope and standing in your belief that God is there.*

Now let's look at the other side of that coin. If we're working on un-failing, we also need to be sure we're helping draw others out of their failures too. We can't leave them on their own. We may not always doubt like Thomas, but how often are we like the other disciples and fail to realize who's missing? How often do we let the Thomases in our midst drift off on their own? It's important to follow Christ's lead by being aware of who's not at the party, who has stopped showing up. It's crucial to find ways to bring them back into the fold, if possible. That is what relationships are all about. That is what God calls us to do. This is key to understanding the example of Jesus being a servant leader. He is a Shepherd seeking to bring the lost lambs home.

TRUST ANYWAY

A final thought comes to us about this passage of Scripture. We are reminded that Judas died by suicide after betraying Christ to the Roman soldiers. (See Matthew 27:5.) Judas wasn't there to see the resurrected Christ, to see the complete revelation. It is easy to write Judas off as the ultimate bad guy who got what was coming to him. However, upon closer examination, we see our own stories reflected in some parts of the accounts of Judas. We have all been untrue to Jesus on our journeys. We think we'd never betray Christ, yet time after time, we find ourselves turning away from those things we know we are to supposed do. We know we are supposed to continue, even if God feels far away, even if it seems as though our efforts are in vain. And we give up. If we are truthful, we will admit that we are more capable of being like Judas than we want to believe.

Yet there is good news found in the story of Thomas. Jesus made that special visit just for him. Jesus wanted Thomas to believe! It is not a stretch to believe that Jesus would have offered that same forgiveness and love to Judas if he had still been around, that He would have welcomed him, thus giving Judas the greatest testimony in history for sharing the good news. Despite Judas's absolute failure in betraying Him, Jesus would have loved him, just as He loves us.

Jesus still reaches out to us with His scarred hands. He invites us to touch. He invites us to believe in a love so powerful that it overcomes deceit with compassion and mends brokenness with relationship. Jesus offers redemption, even today. Even to Judas. Even to us. Even when we can't see the evidence directly around us, He invites us to keep believing and staying strong.

Jesus invites us to believe in a love so powerful that it overcomes deceit with compassion and mends brokenness with relationship.

Thomas teaches us about the sacrificial nature of following Christ. Sometimes we won't see the scars, but we must trust anyway. That is how we turn our failure around. That is how we un-fail.

Christ went to extremes for His followers. There was nothing more important than making sure they understood the message. Jesus walked through walls, He made repeat visits, and He washed the feet of those who would later deny Him. Jesus spent countless hours attempting to teach and mold these fishers of men. Jesus loved and loved; He gave and gave. Jesus wanted His people to get it. He wanted His people to get Him.

As we learn and grow, becoming Christlike is not an easy thing. We must constantly die to self to keep our focus where it needs to be. But we must also live vibrantly to use that focus for the good of others. This isn't as obvious as we'd like it to be. At one point, Thomas was worried about dying with Christ. Then he discovered that Jesus was really calling him to live with Him, to trust and see His goodness, His plan.

EVERY REASON TO BELIEVE

In the end, that encounter with Jesus wasn't just for Thomas. It's also important for each of us today. Without him asking for proof and without Christ's gracious acquiescence, Thomas would have been the lone holdout in Jesus's ministry, a disciple who only saw the death of Jesus. That would have been Thomas's legacy. But Jesus opened Thomas's eyes to the truth, so he was able to reunite with the other disciples and share in their joy.

The disciples all saw Christ and believed in His resurrection. The jury was unanimous. Even in a court of law today, it would be hard to disprove a case with eleven eyewitness accounts! Through all of this, there should be no room for doubt for the rest of us. We can take comfort in Thomas's witness, in his relief. We have every reason to believe, every reason to keep going even when we can't see clearly down the path before us. We have every reason to believe we can un-fail and come out on the other side of failure stronger than we were before.

SCRIPTURE TOOLS

Know now then that the LORD your God is the only true God! He is the faithful God, who keeps the covenant and proves loyal to everyone who loves him and keeps his commands—even to the thousandth generation! (Deuteronomy 7:9 CEB)

Some trust in chariots and some in horses, but we trust in the name of the LORD our God. (Psalm 20:7)

I will say to the LORD, *"My refuge and my fortress, my God, in whom
I trust."*   (Psalm 91:2 ESV)

Trust in the LORD *with all your heart; don't rely on your own intelligence.*   (Proverbs 3:5 CEB)

*"My God sent his angel, and he shut the mouths of the lions. They
have not hurt me, because I was found innocent in his sight. Nor have
I ever done any wrong before you, Your Majesty." The king was overjoyed and gave orders to lift Daniel out of the den. And when Daniel
was lifted from the den, no wound was found on him, because he had
trusted in his God.*   (Daniel 6:22–23)

Don't be troubled. Trust in God. Trust also in me.   (John 14:1 CEB)

*Love bears all things, believes all things, hopes all things, endures all
things.*   (1 Corinthians 13:7 ESV)

REFLECTION QUESTIONS

*Here are some reflection questions you might consider when evaluating and
developing a life of trust:*

1. Thomas wanted to see Jesus in order to believe. Jesus fulfilled
   this request and made Thomas a true believer. Why do you think
   Thomas was specifically motivated to want to touch Christ's
   wounds?

2. Jesus went out of His way to appear for Thomas. In doing so, He
   said, "Blessed are those who believe without seeing." How does
   this speak to us today?

3. Do you believe Jesus would forgive Judas as He had Thomas? What passages come to mind that help inform your answer? How does this possibly give us hope today?

4. How many times are we supposed to forgive those who've wronged us? What can we learn from the example of Christ in this?

5. The Catholic priests found comfort and inspiration from the Saks Fifth Avenue windows as they sought to minister to a hurting city after 9/11. What does this tell us about the humanness of pastors and leaders? As followers of Christ, we are called to be salt and light. That command is not just for those who work in ministry, but for us all. How did Saks Fifth Avenue become Christ to the priests, and how does that inspire you to be Christ for others?

12

LOOKING WITH LOVE

(Acts 9)

We've all made assumptions about others. Judged another person based on their past. Rejected somebody before we got to know them. Refused to really listen to someone else's opinion or what they had to say. We all do it.

And yet, God is asking us to do better. He's asking us to live differently. He might not choose the person we expect to carry out His will, and He might change the heart of someone we thought was stuck in their ways. He might even change us while He's at it. We don't have everything figured out either; God is working on all of us. Who are we to shut down someone else without a second thought, without letting them speak, without giving them a chance? God knows our hearts. He sees what we can't. And even when someone fails horribly, even when it is long-lasting or hurtful, He will still offer them an opportunity for redemption.

God is ready to lead people on the path of un-failing.
We should be right there beside Him,
shining our light into their lives.

We need to start opening our eyes and looking at people in a new way—because God is ready to make changes, to lead people on the path of un-failing. We should be right there beside Him, shining our light into the lives of everyone we know and meet.

THE STORY OF SAUL (AKA PAUL)

Christ's ascension into heaven was followed by the severe persecution of believers, and one person in particular made sure of it. Saul, later known as Paul, *hunted* Christians. An early, brutal example of his participation was the stoning of Stephen. An angry crowd grabbed Stephen and laid their coats at Saul's feet, perhaps because they didn't want their coats covered with Stephen's blood. As the stoning took place, Stephen said, *"Lord Jesus, receive my spirit. ... Lord, do not hold this sin against them"* (Acts 7:59–60.) These words meant nothing to Saul. He didn't stop the stoning, and Stephen died. Saul considered it a win.

He didn't stop there. After that incident, Saul began ravaging the church, scattering believers in all directions. An intellectual man, he'd been well-schooled and held endless passion for his subjects of choice. And now, Saul was passionate about stopping the spread of this new religion that he believed went against the Jewish teachings. He dragged men and women off to prison. There were beatings and deaths. It was a difficult time to be a follower of Christ.

That didn't stop the disciples from spreading the Word. Miracles were still performed, crowds were transformed, and lives were changed. All the while, *"Saul was still breathing out murderous threats against the Lord's disciples"* (Acts 9:1). He was eager to be rid of them entirely.

Cleverly, Saul decided he would go to the high priest to ask for letters to the synagogues in Damascus so that if he found any of Christ's disciples there, he could take them as prisoners to Jerusalem. It was a smart plan, almost guaranteed to expose more Christ followers, and Saul started on his way to Damascus.

Then something totally unexpected happened. As Saul neared the city, a bright light from heaven beamed all around him. It was a powerful, overwhelming sight, and Saul fell hard to the ground.

A voice spoke from out of nowhere. "Saul, Saul! Why do you persecute Me?"

Huddled on the ground, Saul was shaken. "Who are You, Lord?" he cried out.

"I am Jesus, the one you are persecuting," the voice said.

This statement was delivered dramatically, powerfully, because Jesus knew Saul. He knew the passion in Saul's spirit. And Jesus knew that only something remarkable would truly grab Saul's attention and prompt the change that needed to happen.

> *Jesus knew the passion in Saul's spirit. Only something remarkable would prompt the change that needed to happen.*

The voice of Jesus continued, *"Now get up and go into the city, and you will be told what you must do"* (Acts 9:6).

Saul had not been traveling alone. His frightened companions stood speechless. They heard the great voice but could see no one. Saul could see no one either—literally. As he rose from the ground and opened his eyes, there was only darkness. He had been blinded by the light. Saul's companions had to lead him by the hand into Damascus.

Saul was blind for three days, and it was quite a time of reflection for him. He had encountered the very Person he fought against. Now, sitting in the dark, Saul contemplated the many deeds he had committed. How wrong he had been! He ate nothing and drank nothing. All he could do was think and wait.

Meanwhile, there was a disciple in Damascus named Ananias. The Lord appeared to him in a vision and said, "Ananias, go to the house of Judas and deliver a message to Saul of Tarsus. Saul is praying now, and he's seen a vision of you coming to lay hands upon him so that he may regain his sight."

Ananias was a little worried. He wasn't sure he wanted to go visit this killer of Christians. "Lord, I've heard a lot about this guy. He's done so much evil to Your followers in Jerusalem. He'll throw me in jail!"

The Lord said to Ananias, "Go! *This man is my chosen instrument to proclaim my name to the Gentiles and their kings and to the people of Israel. I will show him how much he must suffer for my name*" (Acts 9:15–16).

That was good enough for Ananias. He followed the Lord's command and went to the house. Placing his hands on Saul, he said, "Brother Saul, the Lord Jesus appeared to you and has sent me to restore your sight. He wants you to be filled with the Holy Spirit." Immediately, something like scales fell away from Saul's eyes and his sight was restored. Literally and figuratively, Saul could now truly see. He got up and was baptized, then ate heartily to regain his strength.

Now born again, Saul spent several days with the disciples in Damascus. It was a strange time for them. Here was their persecutor walking and talking among them, now appearing to be on board with the movement, the Way of Jesus Christ. He was *joining* them? They found themselves teaching Saul the very message he had sought to destroy. Within a few days, Saul began to proclaim Jesus to anyone who would listen, declaring, "He's the Son of God!"

It wasn't just the disciples who were startled by this transformation. Everyone had known of Saul's zeal against these men and their God. Now, here he was, shouting their message from the rooftops. It was a shocking political flip-flop.

"Isn't that the guy who killed those believers in Jerusalem?" they asked. They were skeptical and afraid of what might happen. They wondered if it was some diabolical scheme to bring the believers back to Jerusalem in chains. Nonetheless, Saul taught the gospel and grew bolder. He confounded all the Jews in Damascus by proclaiming the Messiah.

It was too much for the religious leaders to handle, too bizarre for them to accept, so they did what they always seemed to do when confronted by someone they could not understand: they began plotting to kill Saul. They watched the gates day and night. Lookouts were placed as they planned an ambush. It was their turn to continue the tradition Saul had started—killing the believers and stopping the spread of the gospel. Saul was just on the other side of the fight now.

The disciples got word of the danger and helped Saul escape so that he could journey to Jerusalem to meet up with the disciples there. However, they did not believe he was now a believer, and they were rightly afraid of Saul. They suspected this was some sort of trick. Things were tense.

Yes, Saul claimed he had been chosen by Jesus Himself. He even had companions who backed his story. But this man, they reasoned, had done so much harm. He had schemed over ways to kill Jesus's followers, threw them in prison, slyly sought them out. It was some time before they allowed themselves to accept him. Only when Saul spoke boldly before crowds in the name of the Lord, only when Saul placed his own life in danger, did the disciples truly believe Saul had been transformed. They sent Saul to Tarsus, and the church's numbers increased greatly.

The disciples finally believed Saul had been transformed when he boldly preached the good news of Jesus, putting his own life in danger.

There is a misconception that God changed Saul's name to Paul in the conversion experience, yet this is not the case. Saul had strong Jewish heritage but was also a Roman citizen. The name *Saul* comes from his Jewish background; *Paul* was a name more closely recognized by his gentile side. In a later communication to the church at Corinth, Paul wrote:

> *Though I am free and belong to no one, I have made myself a slave to everyone, to win as many as possible. To the Jews I became like a Jew, to win the Jews. To those under the law I became like one under the law (though I myself am not under the law), so as to win those under the law. To those not having the law I became like one not having the law (though I am not free from God's law but am under Christ's law), so as to win those not having the law. To the weak I became weak, to win the weak. I have become all things to all people so that by all possible means I might save some. I do all this for the sake of the gospel, that I may share in its blessings.* (1 Corinthians 9:19–23)

Saul allowed even his name to be an instrument in winning people to Christ. Therefore, as his fame grew in the spreading of the Word, he became mostly known by the name of Paul.

Eventually, Paul was commissioned and sent off by the group of believers to preach. He was a powerhouse. Accosted by a magician in Paphos, Paul proclaimed him a son of the devil and called down blindness upon the man, a scene that drew others to Christ. Paul cajoled, argued, and witnessed with the same passion he had once used against this message of hope. Imprisoned in dramatic fashion in Philippi, Paul and Silas sang hymns with such gusto that they literally brought the house down—the prison shook to its foundations in a massive earthquake, the doors cracked open, and the chains fell off the prisoners. Paul greatly influenced the course of Christianity and through his letters, he helped shape the delivery of the good news for all time. Everything he did was done in a big, passionate way.

Paul's new passion could have been hindered and not nearly as influential if the disciples had turned him away and refused to accept him. If they'd failed to protect him. If they'd let their doubts take over instead of giving him a chance to prove himself. If the disciples had focused on Paul's earlier failure, the world would have missed out on so many miracles and countless people would not have heard the good news.

THE UNEXPECTED MESSENGER

It is never fun to end a relationship. It can feel like failure. There is an acknowledgment that some element of brokenness exists that cannot be fixed. Ending a relationship is a difficult process that people may put off for months or even years.

Starting a relationship, on the other hand, is an entirely different matter. There is often a sense of hope. A new friendship or romantic relationship brings with it new ideas and new possibilities. It can boost energy and excitement, especially when things go well from the start. It can feel like the future is bright, and it's quite thrilling.

But what about your other relationships, the ones you maintain over time? What about the people who have stood by you, prayed with you, through thick and thin? How do you continue to honor those friendships over the course of your life?

Now imagine a situation in which you decide to start a new relationship and become friends with someone who previously killed some of your other friends after hunting them down. Are you getting the picture? Doesn't that sound insane?

This is the same predicament the early church was in when the apostle Paul joined them. He had harmed so many believers and had threatened all of their lives. How could they possibly trust him? What if it was all an act? What if this conversion was a ploy to trap and destroy more of those who believed? Make no mistake about it, this was a huge act of trust on the part of the disciples. Yet they trusted. And it literally made a world of difference.

The truth is that God sometimes chooses unexpected messengers. He selects people based on a different rubric than the rest of us. Jesus chose to draw Paul to Himself on the road to Damascus. Can God use a murderer? Though it's hard for us to comprehend, it is not difficult for God. He saw past the sordid deeds of Paul to see what he *could* be. God saw what could be done through Paul, because along with transforming Paul, God knew that love could also change all of humankind. Jesus knew the potential of this man. He knew that Paul would have a zeal beyond anything the disciples had experienced.

Had these followers of Christ never accepted the ministry of Paul, there would've been a great schism in the early church. Perhaps history would've been quite different. It was important for these followers to trust Jesus, their leader. It was necessary to have faith that God is a big God, that His ways are vast, miraculous, and mysterious. They had to let God be God, which meant accepting Paul when God gave him to them.

> *God saw past Paul's sordid deeds to what he could be. He knew Paul would have a zeal beyond anything the disciples had experienced.*

God can use anyone at any time. And that can be a hard pill to swallow. So hard, that many times, we fail to accept what He's doing.

A MESSAGE FOR EVERYONE

Complete 180-degree turns, absolute changes of heart and lifestyle, are abundant in history and literature and continue to be promisingly prevalent in the world today:

- John Newton, the famous English slave trader, went from renowned slave ship captain to remorseful abolitionist. He helped found an anti-slavery society, testified against slavery in Parliament, wrote about it so others could understand the horrors, and preached against it up until his death.

- Celebrity and comic Tim Allen served time in federal prison for drug trafficking and even after his release still struggled with alcohol addiction. He eventually got sober and was able to continue to bring laughter to people across the world. Allen is also involved in the national YMCA, Habitat for Humanity, Special Olympics, and other charities.

- Actor Robert Downey Jr. similarly found himself in rehab for addiction after hitting rock bottom very publicly. He credits his sobriety as the reason he was able to become both an onscreen superhero as Iron Man and a real-life one, visiting children's hospitals to raise kids' spirits and fighting to reduce carbon footprints around the world through the FootPrint Coalition.

All three men turned their lives around completely. All three men initially seemed like a lost cause. There are no limits to what God can do, no limits on who God can change or who He can use.

Do we believe and live this? Do we look outward, seeking the sheep tangled in the briars? Do we truly see the people around us? God chose a murderer of Christians to take His message global. What might He want to do through us? What might He want to do through others, the ones who are hard to love?

We must remember that Jesus knew about the betrayal of Judas before it even happened. And yet Jesus washed his feet anyway. Jesus served this man who would do the unthinkable. Christ loved His enemies and did good to those who sought to persecute Him.

The moment God chooses Paul is the moment that the whole New Testament changes, moving from disciple-centered to a Pauline model wherein Paul diminishes himself to proclaim Christ. Paul does not even talk about meeting Jesus on the road to Damascus in his epistles. We know of it only because Luke shares that wonderful story in Acts 9.

Paul had obviously been a strong and dynamic leader because he led the killing parties. He had always had followers and a mission, but there was a change when Paul began his ministry. Once someone who depended on his own strength and power, as a believer, Paul now stressed his own weakness and Christ's strength making up for his lack. He spoke of his thorn in the flesh. He was no longer the Pharisee with all the answers. He was a humbled man of God. He was a servant for the cause of Christ. He mentored young leaders like Timothy, and he used his influence to spread the Way to entirely new audiences. For Paul, it was about lifting others up and proclaiming the gospel message.

Paul's conversion is significant because he took the news worldwide—specifically to the gentiles. This influx of new blood transformed the entire church. Paul's conversion set into motion the idea that an unconditional God can change the heart and life of *anyone*.

> *We have all fallen short of the glory of God. We all need a Savior to shine His light of love down upon us.*

We are all sinners and have fallen short of the glory of God. We all need a Savior to shine His light of love down upon us to remove the scales from our eyes. Paul might have gotten it wrong for the first part of his life, but the beautiful transformation that took place inside of him rewrote his story. He changed the world for Christ. It is almost impossible to overestimate the influence Paul's journey had on world history.

WILLING TO WORK ON RELATIONSHIPS

The 2016 presidential election process was one of the ugliest political fights in our nation's history. On every front, there was divisiveness. Angry words and hateful sentiments were broadcast daily, while social media separated friends in unprecedented ways. Donald Trump's supporters were at odds with Hillary Clinton's supporters. The Democrats were at odds with the Republicans, and both parties were also at odds internally. There appeared to be no common ground, and opposing sides were viewed as enemies. People from both sides spewed forth hatred and vitriol—including Christians.

The apostle Paul speaks of bringing in nonbelievers by refusing to do anything that would be a stumbling block to them accepting Christ. (See Romans 14:13.) Think about what that means when it comes to responding to the people around us, especially people who don't believe in God! Paul knew that showing someone the Way of Christ is far more important than getting one's view across or having one's opinion heard. Showing someone Christ is about being the hands and feet of Jesus in a harsh world. It is about showing love to a world desperate for communion and belonging, regardless of victories or defeats.

It is our duty, as American citizens, to be united in heart and spirit even if our politics differ. How many people were *unfriended* and cast aside during the 2016 and 2020 election seasons? How many friendships were lost? How much anger even now engulfs our everyday lives to the point that it affects cherished relationships in an adverse way? How much did each of us lose in this process?

As Christians, we should be leaders in accepting others unconditionally and showing them kindness and consideration. We need to start opening our hearts. We need to start seeing people the way God does. For all we know, we might be the person who God is trying to meet on the road to open our eyes and turn our life around.

It doesn't mean we have to accept and believe the same things. It does mean, however, that we should care more about people than about how their beliefs do or don't line up with our own. We should be helping people unite, not creating divisions. Our example should be one of hope and nurturing relationships, not throwing them away.

> *We should be helping people unite. Our example should be one of hope and nurturing relationships, not throwing them away.*

When he was president, Abraham Lincoln filled his cabinet with political opponents. Doris Kearns Goodwin's insightful book *Team of Rivals*[29] explores the fascinating transformation of these *enemies* into teammates and, eventually, ardent supporters of the president. It is a poignant glimpse of an amazing leader who won over a tough group of opponents. Lincoln gathered them close, and his attitude and inclusiveness changed them. Lincoln saw potential in these men. He knew that getting his own agenda moving forward would require compromise and connection. Lincoln literally fought to keep the United States united. He was the right man at the right time.

---

29. Doris Kearns Goodwin, *Team of Rivals: The Political Genius of Abraham Lincoln* (New York: Simon & Schuster, 2005).

Lincoln was a national leader in a unique position, but there is much we as Jesus followers can learn from his example. Being at the same table forces relationship, but first, we must place ourselves in a seat at the table, listen to others, and try to understand them. We can't keep looking at everyone with distrust. We must be willing to learn and grow ourselves. We need to be open to working with other people.

It might not be our job to change or save the whole world. It is our job, however, to make our part of the world a better place by fostering relationships with those around us.

THROUGH EYES OF LOVE AND POSSIBILITY

All of this starts with looking at others through God's eyes, and this is where many of us don't even realize our handicap. From the beginning, when the serpent destroyed the harmony of Eden, scales have been a part of the picture for humans. Like Saul, scales have covered our eyes, blinding us and making our journey difficult and dangerous. How many atrocities have been committed by those who cannot see clearly, who are following their own agenda and can't distinguish the truth?

The greatest impediment to our moving forward and showing love and service to those around us are the scales on our own eyes. We don't see people with God's heart but with our own clouded judgment—a combination of our upbringing, politics, history, personal scars, and so many other things that don't make up our potential.

Sometimes it's the scales of fear that keep us looking inward. We stay within our churches and organizations, scared of the fast-changing world and the people we might meet who are *different*. It is more comfortable to focus on ourselves and find those like-minded around us to join in a holy huddle. It is risky to look outward into our communities to try to find ways to serve.

But we are *called* to look out, to seek and find those who are lost. We are called to remove those scales and truly hunger to see the world around us through the eyes of love and possibility. When the scales fall, it can be a dramatic revelation of God's love.

God changed Saul. He can do big, big things. God is still in that business today. But it is *His* business. All we can do is keep our eyes open and our spirits ready for genuine hearts that are ready to learn and grow. Instead of looking for the failures, we must look for selfless hearts that are ready to change the world for the better, even if it doesn't match what we were expecting.

TIME TO SEE

There is recurring redemption offered through the grace of Jesus Christ. No matter the sin, no matter the wrong, Jesus is always standing ready to shine the light of forgiveness. Paul encountered that light quite literally. And that light is there somewhere in each of our own stories, lighting our way home. Some have seen it and have walked in new directions because of it. Some have turned away from that light and still wander in their dark brokenness. Regardless, Christ is always there with a storehouse of compassion, wishing to help us truly see.

What scales are covering your eyes? What beliefs, sins, fears, or mindsets prevent you from laying it all down and serving the one true King? God has a mission for you. He has bigger things in mind than you could ever imagine, and He is calling you to Him, to serve, love, and change. Allow Him to move through you to change the world. Ask Him to help you see others with compassion, to see their true heart and potential.

> *God is calling you to serve, love, and change.*
> *Ask Him to help you see others with compassion,*
> *to see their true heart and potential.*

It's time to look at people with love, patience, and kindness and welcome them with open arms, even when our views and lifestyles differ. It's time to see the possibility in others, let them into our hearts, open our ears, and listen to what they have to say. It's time to leave the old way of living behind and turn to the Way wholeheartedly, as Saul did. This is the path to un-failing. This is how we win the world for Christ.

SCRIPTURE TOOLS

I will dwell on your mighty acts, my Lord. Lord, I will help others remember nothing but your righteous deeds. (Psalm 71:16 CEB)

A generous person will prosper; whoever refreshes others will be refreshed. (Proverbs 11:25)

Therefore anyone who sets aside one of the least of these commands and teaches others accordingly will be called least in the kingdom of heaven, but whoever practices and teaches these commands will be called great in the kingdom of heaven. (Matthew 5:19)

For if you forgive other people when they sin against you, your heavenly Father will also forgive you. But if you do not forgive others their sins, your Father will not forgive your sins. (Matthew 6:14–15)

He said to them, "Listen carefully! God will evaluate you with the same standard you use to evaluate others. Indeed, you will receive even more." (Mark 4:24 CEB)

"What sorrow awaits you Pharisees! For you are careful to tithe even the tiniest income from your herb gardens, but you ignore justice and the love of God. You should tithe, yes, but do not neglect the more important things." (Luke 11:42 NLT)

Paul and Barnabas remained in Antioch, where they and many others taught and preached the word of the Lord. (Acts 15:35)

REFLECTION QUESTIONS

Here are some reflection questions you might consider when evaluating and developing a life of looking outward:

1. Is there anything God cannot do? Is there anyone God cannot love and forgive? Why do we find it so difficult to love everyone? What can we learn from the story of Paul?

2. Being salt and light to others is our call. Jesus lived this out and washed the feet of His followers. What specific ways can we show a heart for others today? What demonstrations of love could change our own communities, and what stops us from doing these? What commitments can you make today to share God's love with others?

3. Have you truly had a conversion experience? Who has mentored or guided you since? Are there people you trust who might help guide your next steps? What is keeping you from seeking guidance?

4. Paul's conversion shows us that God is willing to use anyone. How does this take away our excuses for not being used for good? What does this say about how much God loves every one of us? How can living in this knowledge change our lives?

5. How can our churches and organizations remove the scales that cover our eyes? What examples can you find, both in your community and beyond, of others who have successfully placed their focus on serving others? What can you learn from them? In what way might partnerships be made?

A FINAL WORD: UN-FAILING INTO WHOLENESS

Anthony Thaxton

We can now start to get it right when we have gotten it wrong. We can pick ourselves up off the floor, admit that we missed the mark, refocus on what we *can* control, look to God, and start *un*-failing. Start using our time on the ground as time to reflect. Then we can take those situations that feel like the end, learn from them, and move forward maybe just a little bit wiser, a tiny bit more aware, and a tad bit closer to God. We're not always going to get it right so we need to start learning how to use those times we get it wrong to sharpen ourselves.

Our society has warped definitions of success and failure. They are woven into the fabric of who we are as Americans. Success is *the American way*. We're told, "You can achieve anything if you only set your mind to it." We are taught from childhood that being a success means earning more, achieving more, *being* more. We carry a strong awareness of our strengths and weaknesses into our adult lives. For most of us, it is not acceptable to simply *be*. We must *be successful*.

I hope Shane and I have shed some light on how failure is part of the journey and how our measure of success is wildly off base.

Society throws platitudes at us. There is a good chance that you, dear reader, can recall some inspirational quote that made you feel pressured rather than inspired. You might work in an office building with motivational posters proclaiming that failure is an event, not a person. They may depict some rugged individual climbing a very steep mountain, a scene where failure—of ropes, equipment, or nerve—would indeed be a tragedy. The picturesque scene is meant to be a metaphor for each of us, to tell us that we can climb those mountains in our life even if adversity comes our way.

But these concepts are more complicated than the idea that we can eliminate the negative by accentuating the positive. The negative is here to stay, and we need to learn how to work with it. Figuring out that success really means focusing on our journey is one of life's big realizations. Success is a mindset. Success is accepting that failure is part of the journey and the reason we do things differently the next time around. If we never really embrace that idea, then we can never truly live in peace.

Success is about being whole. This sounds pretty simple, right? In some ways, it is. However, we try to complicate it by adding markers on the path:

- If I make this much money…
- If I achieve this degree of fame…
- If I rise to the top of my profession…
- If I earn a higher degree…

- If I'm inducted into the Hall of Fame...

- If I win the award...

- If ... if ... if ...

The list can go on and on. In fact, it's a lot easier to write that list than it is to achieve the items on it. Success becomes about doing. Being. Earning.

Framed that way, success is elusive. But that's not the framework for success that we have explored in this book. As we've seen, true success is simply about being whole. And being whole is a journey. We have foundational aspects of failure that we need to understand and recognize so we can stop feeling stunted and effectively start using our failures to learn. Once we can accept our failures and the fact that failure isn't going away, we can take steps to both prevent it, when possible, and learn about ourselves, the world around us, and our relationship with God.

When we realize that un-failing is a steady part of our journey, we can see our lives in a new light, with eyes open to the possibilities of the freedom we can live in and our endless potential. It's not a one-step process that we get to breeze over. It's a constant journey of building, learning, adding, taking away, remaking ourselves, and just getting closer to wholeness with Christ. At its core in Scripture, the conversation about being whole is about taking up our cross, following Jesus, and being Christ to others.

The Bible is often perceived as a complex rule book. Yet it's a road map through life, a blueprint for living. The world was very different when the Bible was written. Most people wouldn't necessarily think of the Book as a guide for success. But we hope that in *this* book, we've shown quite the opposite. The common view is that the Bible tells us what we can't have. (Prosperity gospel teachers are the big exception to this philosophy; we'll have to save that for another book!) The Bible does show God favoring Joseph, David, and Solomon in the Old Testament, but to some, it seems that the New Testament teaches us to give up everything— including that elusive idea of *success*—to simply follow Christ. Or to follow Christ simply. We're not convinced that is the only essential mandate. We see believers being successful because they're sharing good news, sharing resources, and sharing life as they go.

Thus, our take is a little bit different. We feel the Bible says a great deal about success, about what it means to find the other side of failure, and we have tried to share that with you. Like most things, it is how you look at it, but the lessons are there. We can't have success without some failure. We can't begin to understand success without understanding failure and what it can mean to us. Knowing they go hand in hand—really *knowing* this and taking it to heart—can be such a relief. Because our lives aren't about avoiding failure or marking off the checkboxes to success; our lives are about the journey of becoming whole.

It is often hard for many of us to be still. To be quiet. To behave. To be broken. *To just be.* But it doesn't have to be hard for us. Throughout Scripture, God tries to teach us the importance of reflecting on the fact that we belong to Him. He wants us to be in Him. With Christ, we find rest. We find value. God uses the adversity, the failures, to point us back to the fact that true success is finding our worth and place in life in Him.

Sometimes, we end up making our path much more of a struggle than it needs to be. The many lessons in Scripture—of shortcomings, mistakes, disobedience, loss, and failure—teach us many valuable truths that we need to understand. If success is about being whole, failure is about brokenness. Whether it's from a lack, something overdone, or some kind of destruction, it is marked by the absence of wholeness. And we're not going to find that completeness while we're here on earth, so there is going to be brokenness, there is going to be failure. But being prepared to use that failure and build on it can make all the difference in our lives. We need to be ready to un-fail, to use our experiences and grow.

Ecclesiastes 3:11 states, *"He has made everything beautiful in its time."* All of our attempts, all of our failures, are woven into God's plan. He can do something great with them if we let Him. Our broken lives can be made beautiful, even through the brokenness.

So here we are at the end of our time together. Where do you find yourself? Are you beside the road of your life, out of control and in a ditch? Do you find yourself needing to understand how you arrived at where you are? Do you need a gentle Savior to take you into His arms so you can simply rest in Him? Do you need to return to certain stories that spoke to you? Do you need to share some insights with a friend? Do you need to make a phone call you've been putting off for far too long?

We all come to this place with weary hearts, all of us seeking a way to understand ourselves better, yearning to feel as though we have arrived home. It's hard to go through the failures; they're painful to rehash. It hurts to realize how wrong we have been. Even reading the cautionary tales found in Scripture can be a tough experience.

In fact, Shane and I saw quite a few failures while writing this book. We missed deadline after deadline. We changed direction time and time again. We agonized over what lessons to include and what we truly wanted to say. What started out as a quick project turned into a three-year adventure that gave us many insights into our own current challenges. This book helped inform our own lives as we prayerfully wrote and compiled the lessons. What looked like a failure to deliver a manuscript on time has turned into the work you now hold in your hands. It grew deeper the longer it marinated. There is always something better on the other side if you know how to look for it.

Learning how to get it right when we got it wrong, how to un-fail by handing our failures over to a God who makes all things work together for good (see Romans 8:28), can make all the difference in our lives. That's what we intended to explore in this work. That's the journey we've made. We're so thankful you joined us.

Grace and peace to you!

Anthony Thaxton

ACKNOWLEDGMENTS

From Anthony:

Thanks go to:

My coauthor, Shane Stanford—my life has been richer for working with you.

My encouraging friends, Steve Casteel, Maxie Dunnam, Jay Frazier, Chip MacGregor, Donnie Cook, and John Anderson.

The fantastic Whitaker team for their care and support.

My agent and friend, Chip MacGregor of MacGregor Literary.

The JourneyWise family, especially Bill & Carole West and Jack & Betty Moore for their generosity.

Robert St. John, Dr. Blake Thompson, and the crew at the The Institute for Southern Storytelling at Mississippi College. We've got lots of inspiring stories to tell!

Bryan Presson and Mark Simpson—you taught me to "fan the flame." It made all the difference in my life. "If you could do anything in the world for Christ, what would it be?" Indeed!

My mother Linda Thaxton, Ace & Nan Bryant, Michele & Brad Seal, Noah & Reagan Bryant, Ava & Ali Bryant, M. D. & Marijane Whitfield—I hit the jackpot having you in my life, and I love you all dearly.

My wonderful children, Bryant and Sydney—You both are the best things I've ever done.

Amy—My rock, my strength, my passion, my love. Thank you for this wonderful life.

And finally, thanks to Jesus—You take our failings and make us whole. You are the light of the world!

———

From Shane:

The journey that unveiled the heart of this book started in unusual places and experienced many turns along the way. It is only through the patience of those who mean so much to me, both personally and professionally, that what we read together in these pages came to be. I have no other words but "thank you," especially for my coauthor and dear friend, Anthony Thaxton—truly one of the best and most creative people God ever made. As always, there are those for whom my debt of gratitude is too much to repay. And yet they stand by me, cheer me on, and say the right things at the right moments so that what God is pulsing in my heart might land on the page. They are as much responsible for what you read as I am. Thank you for your continued patience and support. I can't say enough about working for such good, godly people. Your counsel and support continue to set the boundaries for where the path leads. You are dear and treasured friends.

To my Moore-West and JourneyWise family: Thank you for making us feel so welcome and at home.

To Sarai Grace (Wes), Juli Anna (Jonathan), Emma Leigh, and Timothy: Thank you for reminding me that God makes more of us than we deserve and blesses us more than we could have imagined. I love you.

To Pokey: No matter how many times I say it, you are my treasure, my heart, and my life—a picture more beautiful even than ... words.

To Jesus: I stand amazed at what You make beautiful. I stand in awe of how You do it. I love You.

ABOUT THE AUTHORS

Dr. Shane Stanford is the founder and CEO of the Moore-West Center for Applied Theology, as well as the president of JourneyWise, the Moore-West Center's faith-based media network. He previously served as a pastor and church planter for more than thirty years. Most recently, he was the sixth senior minister of Christ United Methodist Church in Memphis, Tennessee. He also served as host of *The United Methodist Hour*, a television and radio ministry reaching more than thirty million homes nationwide.

Stanford was awarded an honorary doctorate in divinity from Asbury Seminary in 2014. He also holds a Master of Divinity degree in theology and ethics from Duke University Divinity School, where he won the prestigious Jameson Jones Award in homiletics. He has traveled extensively, sharing his personal testimony as an HIV- and hepatitis-C-positive hemophiliac, husband, father, and pastor.

Stanford has appeared on several media outlets, including *Good Morning America*, *Fox & Friends*, CNN, and Canada's Harvest TV. An accomplished author, he has written numerous books, including *JourneyWise: Redeeming the Broken & Winding Roads We Travel*; *Cure for the Chronic Life* (with Deanna Favre); *A Positive Life*; *When God Disappears*; *Making Life Matter*; *Five Stones: Conquering Your Giants* (with R. Brad Martin);

Mosaic: When God Uses All the Pieces; and *What the Prayers of Jesus Tell Us About the Heart of God*. He is married to his high-school sweetheart, Dr. Pokey Stanford, and they have three daughters and two sons-in-law.

———

Anthony Thaxton is an Emmy Award-winning filmmaker, television producer, and painter. He directed the acclaimed documentary *Walter Anderson: The Extraordinary Life and Art of the Islander*, directed projects with Morgan Freeman and Dolly Parton, and is the producer of *Palate to Palette* on public television.

Thaxton is a founding partner in the Southern Storytelling Institute at Mississippi College, where he was named the 2019 Distinguished Art Alumnus of the Year.

He is the owner of Thaxton Studios, a thirty-year production company whose work includes numerous corporate, government, educational, inspirational, political, commercial, and short film projects, including shows featuring Thaxton's skills as a painter and illustrator.

His photography has been featured on *Good Morning America*, CNN, and *Fox & Friends*, and his vibrant watercolors have been featured in books and on numerous television programs.

He and his wife, Amy, live in Raymond, Mississippi. They are the parents of two grown children, Bryant and Sydney.